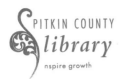

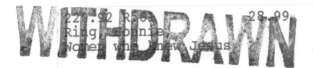

BONNIE RING

WOMEN WHO KNEW JESUS

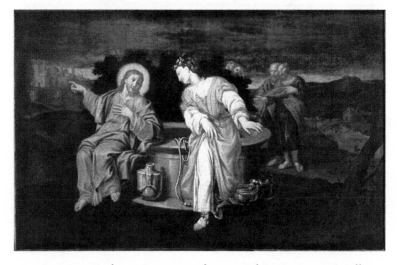

Image 1: Padua – Painting of Jesus and Samaritan at well

authorHOUSE®

AuthorHouse™
1663 Liberty Drive
Bloomington, IN 47403
www.authorhouse.com
Phone: 1 (800) 839-8640

*This book is a work of non-fiction. Unless otherwise noted, the author and the publisher
make no explicit guarantees as to the accuracy of the information contained in this book
and in some cases, names of people and places have been altered to protect their privacy.*

Published by AuthorHouse   09/28/2015

ISBN: 978-1-5049-2925-7 (sc)
ISBN: 978-1-5049-3225-7 (hc)
ISBN: 978-1-5049-2924-0 (e)

Library of Congress Control Number: 2015913338

Print information available on the last page.

*Any people depicted in stock imagery provided by Thinkstock are models,
and such images are being used for illustrative purposes only.
Certain stock imagery © Thinkstock.*

This book is printed on acid-free paper.

*Because of the dynamic nature of the Internet, any web addresses or links contained in
this book may have changed since publication and may no longer be valid. The views
expressed in this work are solely those of the author and do not necessarily reflect the
views of the publisher, and the publisher hereby disclaims any responsibility for them.*

CONTENTS

To all the women who have walked with me as we discovered the women who knew Jesus and found them to be important companions for their life journey.

PREFACE

Ten years after the first women were ordained priests in the Episcopal Church, I began seminary. My first course in church history called for the composition of five meditations on saints of the early church. When I asked whether I could select five women, Guy Lytle,[1] then a young assistant professor, replied, "If you are able to find five women who are worthy of contemplation from the first five centuries, you are free to select them." When he added that he "could *not* readily identify five such women," his attitude challenged my emerging feminist soul.

It was not difficult to find five saintly women. In fact, David Hugh Farmers, author of *The Oxford Dictionary of Saints* lists thirty-one female saints who lived during the first five centuries. That search led me to Elisabeth Moltmann-Wendel's powerful account, *The Women Around Jesus,* where I was able to identify the central women figures in the life and ministry of Jesus. She also introduced me to the emergence of feminist biblical scholarship. I was immediately drawn to the stories of Mary and Martha of Bethany, and Mary Magdalene because of the importance of their encounters with Jesus and his high regard for them.

My interest in these gospel women coincided with the publication of *In Memory of Her: A Feminist Theological Reconstruction of Christian Origins* by Elizabeth Schussler Fiorenza, which challenged the masculine view of Christian history and theological interpretation. That book identified the patriarchal bias of the gospel narrators, which I never heard about in *any* of my seminary classes and also affirmed my interest in the women who

---

[1]   I am very appreciative of the late Very Rev. Guy Lytle for engendering and supporting this journey while he was a member of the faculty of the Church Divinity School of the Pacific, within the Graduate Theological Union in Berkeley, California.

knew Jesus. Ever since its publication and the wonderful studies of biblical women that have been written since, I (like other women) have been looking back at the women of the past from a different perspective—one that reveals more of their character, commitment, wisdom, and steadfast courage. One clear example of this trend is the greater importance now given to the presence of women at the death, burial, and resurrection of Jesus.

In one of my graduate seminars, "The Gospel of John as Instant Theatre,"[2] Jesus's encounters with others came powerfully alive for me as students transformed John's stories into dramatic presentations. One day, I portrayed Mary Magdalene. When I told the hushed audience about my encounter with the risen Jesus, I felt a deep connection with her and with him. That sense of closeness and intimacy has remained with me. It taught me how effective a reenactment of the stories can be to those who perform and witness them.

Later, in 1990, I was invited to design and facilitate a retreat for the women of Piedmont Community Church in Piedmont, California. While listening to their retreat goals, I was reminded of the women in the life of Jesus and proposed that we focus on the women Jesus knew. A retreat with that name was born out of my discussions with their associate pastor, Rev. Charlotte Russell. Twenty-five years later, I am still introducing women to the women who knew Jesus. For that first retreat, I included the little-known story about the dream of Pilate's wife and her effort to warn Pilate to avoid Jesus, the story of Mary and Martha welcoming Jesus into their home, the conversation with the Samaritan woman at the well, the healing of the hemorrhaging woman, and Mary Magdalene's encounter with the resurrected Jesus at the tomb.

To enable retreat participants to personally engage in the stories, identify with specific women, and compare and contrast their own faith experiences, I incorporated storytelling, dramatizations, guided

---

2   Offered by the Rev. Francis Xavier at the Franciscan School of Theology within the Graduate Theological Union in Berkeley, California, in the spring of 1990.

meditations, reflection questions, and group discussions. I have led many groups through this process. Increasingly, it has become a central part of my mission and ministry. Participant feedback has repeatedly shown me that the women and the retreats about them are valuable for developing faith, inspiring witness, and building community. Inspired by the teachings and writings of Marcus Borg, beginning with a retreat he led called "Jesus as a Spiritual Mentor" in 1992,[3] I have been able to provide an encounter with the living Jesus with those narratives, and it has changed and deepened participants' faith and appreciation of him. My friend and colleague, Rev. Molly Darling, saw the importance of my ministry to introduce the women who knew Jesus even before I did, and she kept encouraging me to expand my audience.

After twenty years of retreat leadership focused on the same six women, participants from the Episcopal Church of Almaden[4] asked me to create a second retreat about the other women who knew Jesus. With their encouragement, I began my study of the rest of the women who had encountered Jesus. To do this, I immersed myself in the stories of nine other women who met Jesus: Simon Peter's mother-in-law, Jairus' daughter, a Syro-Phoenician woman (also known as the Canaanite woman), the widow of Nain, a crippled woman who was bent over, the mother of the sons of Zebedee, a woman accused of adultery, a poor widow who gave everything she had, and a woman who anointed Jesus.

As I presented that retreat for the first time, I realized that my work should not end there; the publication of a book based on my retreats would enable women *everywhere* to share in the company of these women. In preparation, I added the stories of the encounters between Jesus and his mother, Mary, and noticed how differently she is described in the Synoptic Gospels of Mark, Matthew, and Luke compared to the Gospel of John. I also familiarized myself with the many new books about the women

---

3   Before the publication of *Meeting Jesus Again for the First Time*, Marcus Borg led this five-day retreat, sponsored by the Pacific Center for Spiritual Formation, which introduced me to the extraordinary man that Jesus was and the way he engaged with others.

4   Located in the Episcopal Diocese of El Camino Real in San Jose, California.

around Jesus for added insights into the women and to avoid duplication. When I examined the latest research on Mary of Magdala, I discovered the richness of the noncanonical gospels. All of this took time; this book marks the completion of those tasks.

The life of Jesus cannot be fully appreciated without the women who interacted with him. The stories of Jesus's encounters with these women show us how Jesus treated women. He spoke to those who had no voice, touching the marginalized and oppressed. Healed, empowered, affirmed, and forgiven, he set them free. They were made whole and worthy of our remembrance.

I am especially appreciative of two women who have sustained and encouraged me during the writing of this book: my spiritual director since 2000, Sister Jean Sauntry, who steadfastly urged me to keep on keeping on, and my friend and mentor, Cynthia Winton-Henry, cofounder of Interplay and Facilitator of the Hidden Monastery, whose belief in me and encouragement to express my spirit through dance and writing has enriched my life. Among the many friends and colleagues who have supported me on this journey, Rev. Molly Darling and Dr. Judith Berling have been exemplary. Also, the editorial suggestions of AuthorHouse have improved this book enormously.

CHAPTER 1: INTRODUCTION

When the women of today are introduced to the stories of the encounters of Jesus with women, they often recognize their similarity to those women, feel the impact of that similarity, and suddenly regard those women as significant role models and companions for their own journeys of faith and witness. All of us need role models—people whose actions and values are a source of guidance and inspiration. By entering into the stories of these encounters of Jesus with women during his ministry, we are able to know him as they did. In those exchanges, he conveys his compassion and his faith, offers insight and affirmation, and acts in ways that benefit them.

A woman's life was very restricted in the first century. The Hebrew purity codes ruled that the flow of blood made a woman unclean and prohibited her from interacting with others or appearing in public at those times. Similarly, the social mores barred women from interacting with men outside of their family or marriage. Therefore, it is both extraordinary and wonderful that there are so many Gospel stories of women encountering Jesus. He appears to have been unafraid to approach women, to listen to them, to heal them, and to affirm God's acceptance of them.

There are many stories about women in all four Gospels. Although they were often unnamed, these women had convictions about Jesus and a sense of safety with him that surpassed that of his male disciples (who were all called by name and given great authority). These stories reveal that Jesus had an appreciative and supportive relationship with many women, and a sense of social equality existed among his male *and* female followers. Each Gospel story involving a woman reveals a unique human being who approached Jesus cautiously and received him gratefully. Every woman who encountered him went away from him changed. The fact that so many stories have been remembered and recorded—and that the Gospels are filled with stories of women as well as men—is a sign that the history of God's salvation cannot be told without women's active participation.

Some of Jesus's encounters with women occurred because their paths crossed accidentally, such as the Samaritan woman at the well. Others actively sought him out or positioned themselves so that a meeting would take place, such as the saucy, non-Jewish Syro-Phoenician woman (also known as the Canaanite woman) who provoked him to minister to someone who was not a descendant of Abraham. Some of the women sought out Jesus for the healing of a disability, such as the hemorrhaging woman who had suffered for twelve years. Sometimes, when men sought Jesus's assistance, the women associated with those men are mentioned (for example, the daughter of Jairus, Simon Peter's mother-in-law, and the mother of the sons of Zebedee). Some women are only identified by their place of residence, such as the widow from Nain. Only a few of the cited women are called by their given names, such as Mary of Nazareth, Mary and Martha of Bethany, and Mary of Magdela. The descriptions of those named women in the Gospels are the most detailed.

In this book, as well as during all my retreats, I use two very different translations of the New Testament: *The Holy Bible: The New Revised Standard Version (NRSV)*, which represents the best current scholarship and *The Message (MSG)* by Eugene Peterson, which is written in everyday language that enables the reader to hear the stories from a fresh perspective. My inclusion of the Gospel texts within the book is designed to engage the reader in the recorded story. When a story appears in more than one Gospel, I typically choose the version from Mark, which is the earliest recorded Gospel. However, if later accounts add different or additional material, I include that material and explain it. This is especially true of the accounts of Mary of Nazareth, the mother. of Jesus. How she is depicted in the first three Gospels (Mark, Matthew, and Luke—known collectively as the Synoptic Gospels because of their shared sources) differs significantly from the Gospel of John; these differences will be explored in each of the stories that include her.

I believe that God has no gender, and that gender-based references to God are difficult for many women; therefore, I have eliminated gender in all the quoted references to God by placing my choice of a substitute in brackets. I also have substituted the terms *realm of God* and *reign of God* for the gender-based term *kingdom of God*, and they will appear in brackets as well. Similarly, although Jesus was unmistakably a man, he was also a human being and a son of humanity. I use those terms interchangeably, using brackets.

As you read a story, I invite you to take time to visualize it so that you can more fully experience it. This method, which I learned from the Ignatian Spiritual Exercises,[5] engages the reader's participation in a powerful way. I have labeled these experiences *Guided Meditations*.

To further enrich your experience, there are questions for you to ponder and memories of your own to recover, with space provided for your reflections. I hope you will take time to journal your reactions to each of the stories and to reflect on them during times of quiet.

Through this book, I hope you will come to know each of the women that Jesus knew and appreciate their attitudes towards Jesus and his deep insight into them, his compassion for them, and his generosity in sharing his wisdom and healing gifts. You may be surprised to discover how quickly your own stories are evoked by hearing theirs, and how similar you are to one or many of them. In each of the encounters detailed in this book, you will also meet Jesus, perhaps for the first time.[6]

The stories about Jesus are stories that concern relationships. In his relationships with others, we gain a fuller picture of the man. We discover

---

[5] Taught annually at Mercy Center in Burlingame, California, and elsewhere. I experienced the Exercises under the leadership of Jim Neafsey, who was my spiritual director for a decade.

[6] My understanding of Jesus has been profoundly influenced by the insights of the late Marcus Borg and his book, *Meeting Jesus Again for the First Time*. I regret that he didn't live long enough to read this book, which reflects his understanding and appreciation of Jesus.

how forthright and self-assured he was, how trustworthy and attentive, how intuitive and provocative, how complimentary and affirming, how compassionate and empathic, and how principled. We also can notice his full humanity: how abrupt and caustic he can be, how instructive, how directive, and how challenging he is when he disagrees.

Over and over again, Jesus taught the primacy of the commandment to love.[7] Jesus conveys the message that God loves us as we are and asks us to love ourselves and others in the same way. In the love with which God created all living things, each of us was created. To fulfill the commandment to love, we cannot stop with just loving God or our neighbors; we must also love ourselves, not out of egotism, but out of an appreciation for our God-given potential—despite our shortcomings and our need to grow and change. This book is an invitation to know and love yourself as you come to know and love Jesus and the women who knew him. My experiences as a psychotherapist and a priest have shown me that when we are unable to love ourselves, we find it difficult, if not impossible, to believe that God loves us.[8] Similarly, without a full sense that God loves us, we lack the foundation to love ourselves and our neighbors. Jesus's treatment of women demonstrates the breadth and depth of God's love.

Bible stories teach us a lot about God and God's people. Many of the stories can help us see parts of ourselves—both the parts we like and the parts that we would prefer to deny, hide, or eliminate. By looking closely at the women in the New Testament Gospels who encountered Jesus, we can

---

[7]   The primacy of the commandment to love is the central premise of the report of the Diocese of California's Theological Task Force on the 1998 Lambeth Resolution 1.10.d, which stated that "Homosexual practice was incompatible with Scripture," which I cochaired. A *New Testament* Scholar, L. William Countryman, was a vital participant in that group. Their findings are printed in "The California Report" entitled "Holy Relations and the Authority of Scripture," which I coedited.

[8]   The importance of self-love is not only essential to our lives as Christians but it is also foundational to the new emphasis of positive psychology through the practice of mindful self-compassion, as taught by psychologists Kristin Neff and Chris Germer.

gain a clearer sense of our own faith and receive new sources of inspiration and models for growing our spirituality and leading others on their own faith journeys.

As you proceed through these pages, two attitudes will be helpful: a willingness to let these biblical women speak with their own voices and an openness to hearing what you may not have heard before. I believe that these stories can help us uncover more of the richness of our own stories. Our stories are really the most precious things we have.[9] Although they can never be taken from us, they are fragile. We often hide them by swaddling them in protective layers of socially acceptable summaries, armoring the tender parts against invasion, and camouflaging our deepest questions and dreams so brilliantly that sometimes even we can't find them. Often, we become afraid of our stories: afraid of what will happen if we peel away the protection and see for ourselves what is at our core. Let this book take you gently by the hand so that you can unwrap your stories and see them for the sacred wonder that they are. When you are able to see them with love more than fear, you will be able to discover their worth and feel that God is with you and in you. This is profoundly holy work.

If you can organize a small group to take this journey with you, the same activities can be undertaken in a small group setting. It is best to focus on one woman each week for five or six weeks, followed by a break before addressing the other women. The stories published here are chronologically placed insofar as I was able to ascertain the correct order in the life and ministry of Jesus.

The power of each story is enhanced by a photo, painting, or illustration that accompanies each chapter. I am very grateful to Rev. Jeffrey W. Hamilton, the minister of La Vista Church of Christ in Nebraska for permission to use the ones copyrighted by his church from old Children's Bibles. The others were purchased from Thinkstock Photos.

---

[9]   My appreciation of the importance of our stories was developed during a series of fruitful conversations with Rev. Molly Darling who was the first to recognize the significance of my work.

The life of Jesus cannot be told without the women who interacted with him. The stories of his encounters with these women show us how Jesus treated others. He spoke to those who had no voice, especially the marginalized and oppressed. Healed, empowered, affirmed, and forgiven, he set them free. They were made whole and worthy of our remembrance. Jesus is a model for who God is in relation with us, and how we are called to be in relationships with each other. When we really believe that statement, we can believe in ourselves and build the basis for a different relationship with God and Jesus which will empower us to share our messages with the world.

Let us begin our journey.
Blessings.

Please feel free to write me about your experiences with this book and any suggestions you have for its revision at drbonniering@comcast.net

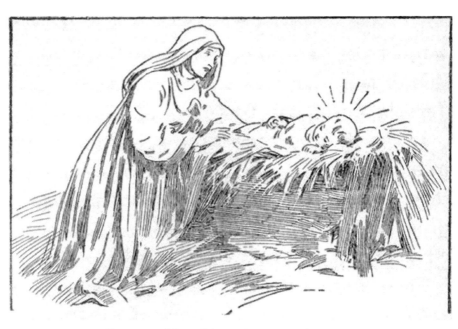

Image 2: Mary Places Jesus in a Manger

CHAPTER 2:
MARY WELCOMES THE BABY JESUS

Our primary images of Mary come from Luke's Gospel, where she is the central figure of his narrative of the birth of Jesus.[10] Mary is amazed to be told that she has "found favor" with God. After all, she is only a young woman: a "nobody" who believes herself to be unworthy of God's attention. However, after the angel's reassurance that God has an extraordinary plan for her, she begins to see herself differently and calls herself "the servant of The Lord,"[11] which is a common phrase in the Hebrew Bible for those chosen by God to be God's agents and spokespersons. It is this reversal in her response to the angel Gabriel that has made Mary revered by the church.

In *The Message*, Eugene Petersen helps us understand her changed attitude by having her say, "I'm the Lord's maid ready to serve."[12] The word for *maid* is *doule*, which refers to an obedient slave, especially a slave who chooses to remain with her master out of love, loyalty, and devotion. It is what the angel didn't say about how her life would change that led Mary to proceed with trust and love for the God that had chosen her. She could not foresee Herod's decree, the flight to Egypt, or the weight of responsibilities that would need to be assumed by such a young girl.

I first met Mary when I was also a young girl. I have long admired her faith, trust, and willingness to accept God's invitation. When I was thirteen, I saw a Christmas pageant for the first time. I heard the ancient prophecies and saw the miraculous story unfold as carols proclaimed the birth of Jesus. When I learned, much later, that Mary's betrothal to Joseph

---

[10]   *NRSV,* Luke 1:26–56; 2:1–20, pp. 56–58. Matthew's nativity story focuses on Joseph.
[11]   Ibid., *NRSV,* Luke 1:38, p. 57.
[12]   *MSG,* Luke 1: 26–28, p. 1862.

meant an engagement to marry and not marriage, and that a pregnant, unmarried Jewish girl was subject to death by stoning due to suspected adultery, my admiration for her courage and commitment grew.

Listen to how Luke's story unfolds:

> The angel Gabriel was sent by God to a town in Galilee called Nazareth, to a virgin engaged to a man whose name was Joseph, of the house of David. The virgin's name was Mary. And the angel came to her and said, "Greetings, favored one! The Lord is with you." But Mary was much perplexed by his words and pondered what sort of greeting this might be. The angel said to her, "Do not be afraid, Mary, for you have found favor with God. And now, you will conceive in your womb and bear a son, and you will name him Jesus. He will be great, and will be called the Son of the Most High, and the Lord God will give to him the throne of his ancestor David. He will reign over the house of Jacob forever, and of his [realm] there will be no end."

> Mary said to the angel, "How can this be, since I am a virgin?" The angel said to her, "The Holy Spirit will come upon you, and the power of the Most High will overshadow you; therefore the child to be born will be holy; he will be called Son of God. And now, your relative Elizabeth in her old age has also conceived a son; and this is the sixth month for her who was said to be barren. *For nothing is impossible with God.*"[13]

> Then Mary said, "Here am I, the servant of the Lord; let it be with me according to your word." Then the angel departed from her.[14]

---

[13]   Emphasis mine. This is the message of the nativity story.

[14]   Op. cit., *NRSV,* LUKE 1:26–38, pp. 56–57.

Guided Meditation

Take a few minutes. Picture Mary being greeted by Gabriel. Imagine her youthful, feminine features.
Notice her reactions of surprise and confusion.

Watch her attitude change as the angel reveals more of God's message. What do you notice?

Now, imagine *yourself* being addressed by an angelic creature that you did not know who insists that *you* have found favor with God. Imagine your reactions to the Angel. How would you respond?

Imagine being confronted by that angel again. This time the angel brings you more unexpected news when he says: "You will serve God even though this has not been your plan."

Imagine having *your* plans changed by an Angel's message. Imagine how *you* would respond to his proposed changes. Describe *your* response.

The Story Continues

Once Mary understands the angel's message and accepts his words, we are presented with a picture of her receptivity to God and her joy:

> "My soul magnifies the Lord, and my spirit rejoices in God my Savior, for [God] has looked with favor on the lowliness of [God's] servant. Surely, from now on all generations will call me blessed; for the Mighty One has done great things for me and holy is [God's] name."[15]

Comments

Throughout the ages, most references to Mary have focused on this unique incident of receptivity and acceptance. The Roman Catholic Church framed her response as obedience. It has so praised and honored her for her submissiveness to God that it has presented her to the world as the model woman.

It is this early Lukan tradition about Mary that has provoked feminist theologians and biblical scholars to see more in Mary than her compliance. Rosemary Radford Reuther, the author of *Mary—The Feminine Face of the Church*,[16] was one of the first to counteract this image of submissiveness by stressing that Mary "is consulted in advance" and actively "gives her consent."[17] She sees Mary as an "active, personal agent in the drama of God's incarnation,"[18] who is "an independent agent cooperating with God in the redemption of humanity."[19] Like many of the other women who encountered Jesus later in his ministry, she is a person who demonstrates courage, strength, and initiative. She accepts the call to bear God's child and rejoices. In Petersen's words, she says:

---

15 Op. cit., *NRSV*, LUKE 1: 46–48, p. 57.
16 Ruether, Rosemary Radford, *Mary—The Feminine Face of the Church*. Philadelphia, The Westminster Press, 1977.
17 Ibid., Ruether, p. 32.
18 Ibid., Ruether, p. 32.
19 Ibid., Ruether, p. 33.

"I'm the most fortunate woman on earth! What God
has done for me will never be forgotten."[20]

I have no idea how many people God has spoken to, but I have
always remembered Joan of Arc's response to the inquisitor at her trial by
church authorities in Jean Anouilh's play *The Lark*: "Doesn't everyone hear
voices?"[21] Those words validate my own experience.

When I was Mary's age, my Dalton High School class attended an
overnight retreat at a Roman Catholic convent. Initially, I found the
austerity of my convent room unsettling; my feelings changed as soon as I
entered the chapel and knelt down. Suddenly, I felt like I had come home!
I sensed that I was in God's presence, which was an experience I had never
had before. The room was silent until the priest spoke. He said, "God has
been waiting for you, to welcome you home." And I knew that the words
were true, that God was there to welcome me with love. I think this was
how Mary felt when the angel addressed her.

God also spoke directly to me. In 1982, seated in church before the
Good Friday service, I heard God say, "I call you!" I was so surprised that
I said nothing. I asked no questions, but I knew something significant had
just happened. Those words were unmistakably clear and audible. I looked
around in search of the source of the voice I heard, but there was no one
else in the church. I wish I had asked, "Who are you?" and "Why me?"
and "What are you calling me to do?" All of those questions emerged later.
My first reaction was excitement: *God spoke to me!* I felt special, honored,
and singled out. I had no doubt that I had heard the voice of God just as
Mary and Joan had. Finally, when I got beyond my pride that God had
spoken to me, I began to wonder what God meant.

---

[20] Op. cit., *MSG*, Luke 1: 47–48, p. 1864.

[21] Jean Anouihl, *The Lark*, translated by Christopher Fry and adapted by Lillian
Hellman for the New York production in 1955, two years after I enrolled at
Dalton High School.

Without stopping to ask God, I quickly assumed that God was calling me to ordained ministry and I reacted strongly and assertively: "Hell no!" I muttered, "I won't go!" I believed that a call to the priesthood involved a change of careers, giving up everything I associated with being myself, and radically altering my life. I tried bargaining with God by saying, "I'll do anything you want as a layperson. I will volunteer my time, contribute leadership, serve as an example, become a witness to God's work—anything but go to seminary for more graduate education in order to become a priest." For four years, I did all those things. Eventually, I became the senior warden of my parish, which is the greatest responsibility a layperson can have in an Episcopal congregation. Yet, inside of me, I still felt unsettled by my refusal to do what I thought God was asking me to do.

And then I attended the first national church conference on AIDS at Grace Cathedral in San Francisco, where I served as a panelist and a discussion group leader. Attendees included clergy, lay caretakers, and individuals suffering with the disease. Many members of my San Francisco parish were dealing with HIV/AIDS, and we were among the first congregations in the Bay Area to seek ways to support them. To listen to their stories and offer God's unconditional love at that conference led me to feel totally congruent for the first time in my life because I was being the person I was called to be. That is when my "yes" began to surface.

Two months later, I was stopped in my tracks by a large Cadillac car as I was taking an afternoon run. When I came to consciousness six hours later, I puzzled over the intent of such an unexpected accident. I wondered whether God had become impatient with me. I took that sign to be a "whack on the side of the head"[22] from God, enabling me to trust God's voice and respond affirmatively. Like Mary, I could not see what lay ahead. I only knew in my heart that I had to do what God was asking of me.

Ten years after I first heard God's voice, I was ordained a priest in the Episcopal Church. It was only then that I asked the important questions:

---

[22] A term popularized by Roger von Oech in 1982, when he published a book by that title.

Why were you calling me? What are you really calling me to do? An answer came back: *I am calling you into a deeper relationship with me!* That has been my life task for the last twenty-two years, and it has changed my life in far deeper ways than adding a new title, new responsibilities, and a clerical collar.

Reflect on Your Experience

Just as Mary pondered God's call, I suggest you stop and ask yourself, *Is God calling me? Have I heard God's voice? Do I hear it now?*

What is God calling you to do? How will you respond?

Conclusions

The call of each of us is a crucial, life-changing moment in our lives. To appreciate Mary, we need a sense of her call as well as any we have received.

Luke's Gospel tells us that, after her visitation by the angel announcing the birth of Jesus (and again after her encounter with Jesus in the Temple), Mary "treasured all these things in her heart."[23] In doing this, she offers us a model of contemplation, which is necessary if we want to understand the direction of God's Spirit in our lives.

---

[23]   Op. cit., *NRSV,* Luke 2:51b, p. 59.

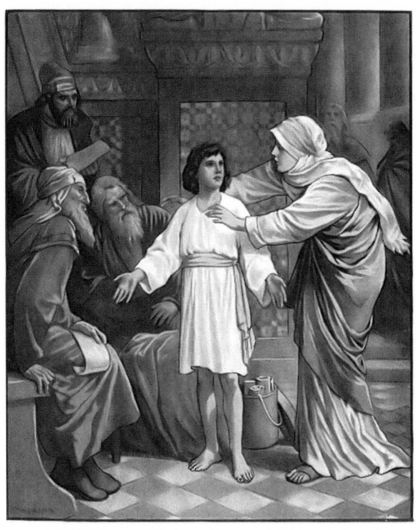

Image 3: Jesus at Twelve in the Temple Discussing God

CHAPTER 3:
MARY FINDS JESUS AT 12
WITH THE TEMPLE ELDERS

Because the New Testament gives no information about Mary's role in Jesus's religious development, Mary Christine Athans has tried to reconstruct the Jewish Mary in her book, *In Quest of the Jewish Mary*. Athans says, "Since Jewish children often learned their first prayers and home rituals from their mothers, it is not unrealistic to assume that Mary would have taught Jesus." [24] We can assume that the Sabbath was observed in Jesus's home and that work was suspended for those twenty-four hours. On Saturday mornings, they probably attended the local synagogue together (if there was one in Nazareth). No remains have been excavated there to validate the existence of a synagogue, but in those days, synagogues were merely outdoor meeting places where Jews gathered to read and discuss the Torah.

Mosaic Law required Jews to make an annual pilgrimage to the Temple in Jerusalem for the feast of the Passover, to commemorate the deliverance of the Jews from the oppression of the Egyptians. At twelve, Jesus was approaching the age of manhood. It was time for him to prepare for his Bar Mitzvah (the Jewish initiation ritual) through a public reading from the Torah scrolls and an offering of his own explanation of its meaning. [25] After four years of weekly attendance at the synagogue, Jesus would have heard enough to cover all the laws and prophets. His ability to impress

---

[24] Mary Christine Athans, *In Quest of the Jewish Mary*, p. 94.

[25] According to Jewish law, when Jewish boys become thirteen years old, they become accountable for their actions and become a bar mitzvah (son of the law). Prior to reaching bar mitzvah, a child's parents hold the responsibility for the child's actions. After this age, boys bear their own responsibility for Jewish ritual, law, tradition, and ethics, and they are able to participate in all areas of Jewish and community life.

the elders in the Temple at age twelve, described here, required significant exposure to Hebrew tradition and wisdom. Luke tells us the following:

> Now every year [Jesus's] parents traveled to Jerusalem for the festival of Passover. And when he was twelve years old, they went up as usual for the festival. When the festival was ended and they started to return, the boy Jesus stayed behind in Jerusalem, but his parents did not know it. Assuming that he was in the group of travelers, they went a day's journey. Then they started to look for him among their relatives and friends. When they didn't find him, they returned to Jerusalem to search for him. After three days they finally found him in the Temple sitting among the teachers, listening to them and asking them questions. And all who heard him were amazed at his understanding and his answers. When his parents saw him they were astonished; and his mother said to him, "Child, why have you treated us like this? Look, your father and I have been searching for you in great anxiety." [Jesus] said to them, "Why were you searching for me? Did you not know that I must be in my [parent's] house?" But they did not understand what he said to them. Then he went down with them and came to Nazareth, and was obedient to them. His mother treasured all these things in her heart. And Jesus increased in wisdom and in years, and in divine and human favor.[26]

---

26 Op. cit., *NRSV*, Luke 2:41–52, p. 59.

Guided Meditation

Become engaged in this story by picturing Mary and Joseph as they join the joyful throng of pilgrims returning home.

Notice how they converse with others as they walk, sharing stories of their experiences of the Passover and time spent with distant relatives and friends.

With so many people gathered along the road, Mary and Joseph do not notice their son's absence. Even as the sun begins to set and food is shared, they assume that Jesus is with his friends or relatives and neighbors. Imagine this scene.

The next morning, as Joseph and Mary prepare to set out again for Nazareth, they look everywhere for Jesus without success.

Feel the deep concern that rises up in them and leads them to decide to return to Jerusalem and look for him there.
Imagine them on the return trek.

During the three days that Mary and Joseph spend searching the city, visiting all the places they had been, their angst grew.

Imagine their fright and apprehension.

Finally, Mary and Joseph go to the Temple searching for Jesus. Imagine their surprise when they find him there conversing comfortably with the elders and teachers.

Notice their reaction: they are not enthralled or captivated; they become upset with him.

Notice how quickly Mary shows her irritation with Jesus. She does not appear to be overjoyed to find him. Instead. Mary's emphasis is on the anxiety that Jesus has caused his parents when they were unable to find him.

Imagine her dismay.and irritation.

Imagine the boy's confusion, when his parents' appear so displeased. with him.

The Message Provides this vivid Picture

The Message provides us with this vivid picture.

> The teachers were all quite taken with him, impressed with the sharpness of his answers, his parents were not impressed; they were upset and hurt. His mother said, "young man, why have you done this to us? Your father and I have been half out of our minds looking for you."[27]

Mary's chastising words remind us of the encounters we have had with our own parents or parent figures, when we have acted independently or disobediently as children or young adults.

Reflection Questions

Did you ever go off independently not expecting to elicit parental concern?

---

[27] Op. cit., *MSG*, p. 1868.

How did your parents react, when they didn't know where you were or couldn't find you?

What happened when you were found?

Was there a time in your own life as a parent, when you became separated from your child?

How did you react?

Were you angry or frightened?

When you found your child, did your reaction change?

Comments

This story demonstrates that Jesus is aware of his life purpose as a young man. When he responds to his mother, Jesus is not contrite or apologetic. Luke presents him as knowledgeable and wise beyond his years at age 12. Jesus sees nothing wrong in his behavior. He keenly understands that he needs to be learning from the Temple teachers, so he wonders why his parents do that expect that as well.

It is here that Jesus first calls God his parent and says that he must be in his parent's house. The term he uses is *Abba*, which conveys an intimate family relationship. The rabbis and teachers are obviously comfortable with Jesus there in the Temple, even pleased with how deeply he understands. But his mother fails to understand his assertion of his rightful place in the Temple. David Redding accurately interprets Jesus's response to mean, "I am not your little boy anymore. Now I belong to God."[28]

Mary sees Jesus through the eyes of a mother whose son has misbehaved and caused her alarm. She ignores the high regard given him by the Temple elders. Her absorption in her own distress prevents her from appreciating Jesus's need to prepare for his role as an agent of God. In this incident, Jesus seems to appreciate the gap; according to Luke, he dutifully returns with his parents to Nazareth and minds his ways.

---

[28]   David A. Reading, *Lives He Touched*, p. 7.

Psychologists often refer to the teen years and young adulthood as a time of *individuation* and *differentiation,* which refers to the ways a maturing youth seeks to both differentiate himself or herself from his or her parents and mark identity characteristics that are uniquely his or hers. I think this is what is going on here: Jesus is claiming his identity as God's child and as a student of God's word. Mary fails to agree when he is twelve, and again, eighteen years later, after he begins his public ministry.

Reflection Questions

Consider your own adolescence. Did you begin to challenge some of your parents' expectations or move in new directions?

Share your similarities to the life of Jesus when you were a teenager.

Mary is using her parental authority. Is that something you have experienced in your parent-child relationships?

How does her behavior make you feel toward her?

My Experience

My acceptance of Christianity during high school led to a unique and distinct identity that differed from my mother's indifference toward religion and the antipathy toward religion that my father expressed, which resulted in a breach that lasted many years. At an interracial and interregional conference of Episcopal youth that I helped organize, he was finally able to connect my dedication to human rights and intergroup relations education with my Christian views and showed strong approval.

Conclusions

I find a real incongruity between Mary's behavior at the birth of Jesus and the only recorded story between the boy Jesus and his Mother, even though both are reported by Luke. When Mary finds Jesus in the Temple at age twelve, her perceptions of his behavior significantly differ from his. One possible explanation for this difference is the widespread belief that the infancy narratives in Luke were written later and have questionable historic validity. Her inability to understand him would make more sense if his birth was not predicted by a messenger from God. That would help explain Mary's belief that Jesus's protracted stay in the Temple was wrong, as was his assurance that his presence there was necessary. I like Luke's birth narrative, as is evident in Chapter 2 of this book, but I cannot ignore the dissimilarity in Mary's behavior in these two stories.

To further complicate our understanding of their relationship, I have found that the Gospel of John presents a very different portrait of their relationship by noting that Mary was the initiator of the first miracle at the wedding in Cana and later appeared at the cross to initiate the birth of the church. As a result, I have highlighted the ways in which John's

Gospel differs from the other three in this instance and throughout later sections of this book.

Clearly, the Gospels are not consistent in their treatment of the relationship of Jesus with his mother, and the difference is worthy of further research and interpretation. I find myself more and more appreciative of the Synoptic Gospels because their agenda is to recount what was known about Jesus; John's agenda, however, is to reveal the signs that show that Jesus is the Messiah.

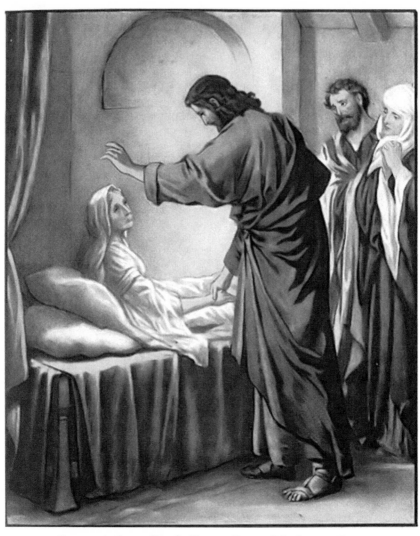

Image 4: Jesus Heals Simon Peters Mother-in-Law

CHAPTER 4:
JESUS HEALS
SIMON PETER'S MOTHER-IN-LAW

The ministry of Jesus in Galilee begins after the arrest of John the Baptist, when he starts to gather his disciples in Capernaum. According to Mark, first he calls the fishermen, Simon Peter and Andrew. After that, he calls Zebedee's sons, James and John. After spending the day teaching in the synagogue there, Jesus left the meeting place and came to Simon and Andrew's house. Mark's account is brief.

> Now after John [the Baptizer] was arrested, Jesus came to Galilee, proclaiming the good news of God, and saying "The time is fulfilled, and the [reign] of God has come near; repent and believe in the good news."

> As Jesus passed along the Sea of Galilee, he saw Simon and his brother Andrew casting a net into the sea—for they were fishermen. And Jesus said to them, "Follow me and I will make you fish for people." And immediately they left their nets and followed him. As he went a little further, he saw James, son of Zebedee and his brother John, who were mending their nets. Immediately, he called them; and they left their father Zebedee in the boat with the hired hand, and followed him.

> They went to Capernaum; and when the Sabbath came, he entered the synagogue and taught. They were astounded at his teaching, for he taught them as one having authority and not as the scribes.[29]

---

[29]   Op. cit., *NRSV*, Mark 1:14–22.

> As soon as they left the synagogue, they entered the house of Simon and Andrew with James and John. Now Simon's mother-in-law was in bed with a fever, and they told Jesus about her at once. He came and took her by the hand and lifted her up. Then the fever left her, and she began to serve them.[30]

Comments

This is the first recorded physical healing[31] in Mark's Gospel. It involves Simon Peter's mother-in-law, who resides with Peter and his wife in their home. We are not told why she is in their house, but we can safely assume that she lives with them either because her husband is dead and she provides services in exchange for housing, or because she is there to assist her daughter, as fisherman work through the night and are thus less available to their wives and children.

After learning of her illness, Jesus goes to her bedside without hesitation and heals her. By entering the room where she lies in bed, he ignores custom and propriety. He greets her, takes her hand, and lends his weight to help her stand. With his touch, she is restored to full health causing the fever to vanish.

Aware that Peter has abandoned his livelihood as a fisherman to follow this man, his mother-in-law does not resist receiving Jesus at her bedside. Throughout her encounter with Jesus, she says nothing. As soon as she experiences his healing power, she leaps up to serve him, which is a central aspect of the ministry of Jesus,[32] and is what he requires of his disciples. Her actions are proof of "the immediacy and completeness of her cure," and her service is a sign that she is eager to offer him hospitality in her son-in-law's home.[33]

---

[30]　Ibid., *NRSV,* Mark 1:29–31.

[31]　Most biblical scholars distinguish this physical healing from an expulsion of demonic spirits.

[32]　Thurston, Bonnie, *Women in the New Testament: Questions and Commentary,* p. 69.

[33]　Getty-Sullivan, Mary Ann, *Women in the New Testament,* p. 72.

Four other healings are performed in Capernaum that day: the curing of a demoniac, the cleansing of a leper, the healing of a paralyzed person, and the restoration of a man with a withered hand. In all cases, the disciples of Jesus are witnesses to the "mighty acts" that Jesus is able to perform, even for the lowest members of society.

Guided Meditation

Let us look closely at Jesus and Peter's mother-in-law.

In the Synagogue, Jesus is forthright and confident. He is assured in his new role as he proclaims the good news of God's love. Imagine him there as their teacher.

Observe Jesus exuding that same confidence and sureness as he approaches the sick woman. As soon as he learns of her illness, he helps her.

See how simple and swift his actions are. Jesus goes to her bedside and reaches for her hand; his touch brings healing, which allows her to stand up with his assistance.

Notice that the healing happens in seconds and there is no exchange of words. Picture this scene.

Imagine yourself as Peter's mother-in-law. Imagine what it feels like to have Jesus touch your hand, cooling your high fever and healing you with his touch.

Imagine Simon Peter's mother-in-law may be unaware of the teachings of Jesus and the ways he will urge his disciples to respond to others with love. But she has a direct experience of his healing powers. Imagine this.

As her fever lifts, her strength returns. Imagine her relief when she recognizes that Jesus has healed her.

Reflection Questions

How do you interpret the actions of Peter's mother-in-law when she jumps up to serve him? Is this an act of gratitude? Or is it the response of a woman with renewed strength who is able to resume her normal duties?

Are her actions an example or model of discipleship for you? Why or why not?

My Experience

In the months following my high school experience of God's welcome at the convent, I toured the major cities in England, France, and Italy with my family. Churches were the central points of attraction. My budding faith grew in the shadows of those sacred sites. After my return, I told a friend of my conversion and asked him to take me to a Sunday church service. Prior to our visit, I accidentally lanced my ankle on a rusty nail. Even after a tetanus shot and special bandaging, it was very painful. He took me to the Episcopal Church of the Heavenly Rest on Fifth Avenue in Manhattan where the Rector, Rev. Dr. John Ellis Large, preached about his experiences in his healing ministry. As I was leaving the church service, I noticed that my foot no longer hurt. I felt healed, and I also felt that my faith had deepened. I became a member of that church and was baptized there.

Reflection Questions

Have you ever had a healing experience like Simon Peter's mother-in-law?

How did you feel afterwards?

What was the first thing you did once you were able?

Healing was a significant part of the ministry of Jesus. What do his healing gifts mean to you?

Do you believe that it is possible for those of us who are Jesus's disciples to heal in his name?

Mark claims that what Jesus did was extraordinary, not what was expected of the Messiah. In what ways does Jesus measure up to or fail to measure up to your expectations in this story?

Differences Among the Three Synoptic Gospel Accounts

The healing of Peter's mother-in-law appears in all three Synoptic Gospels. In Luke's Gospel, the healing occurs before Jesus calls Peter, Andrew, James, and John as disciples. The healing of Simon Peter's mother-in-law results in the calling of Simon. Jesus's assistance is sought, and he speaks to the fever:

> Now Simon's mother-in-law was suffering from a high fever, and they asked him about her. Then he stood over her and rebuked the fever, and it left her. Immediately, she got up and began to serve them.[34]

In Matthew's Gospel,[35] the healing of Simon Peter's mother-in-law occurs much later in Jesus's ministry—after he has performed many healings. Additional healings take place later that day in Peter's house "to fulfill what had been spoken through the prophet Isaiah, 'He took our infirmities and bore our diseases.'"

All these texts highlight the power of Jesus. The Gospel writers have intentionally located them at different times in the ministry of Jesus to emphasize different points. For example, Luke emphasizes the intensity

---

[34] Op. cit., *NRSV*, Luke 4:38b–39, p. 62.

[35] Op. cit., *NRSV*, Matthew 8:17, p. 8.

of the fever; thus, the immediacy of the cure results in Peter's decision to follow Jesus.

Conclusions

This healing takes place in a home, away from the public. "The home is the traditional role of women."[36] it is where most women spent the majority of their time. After Jesus touches and heals Peter's mother-in-law, her immediate response is to resume her duties of hospitality.

In the early church environment, ministry or service to others was described by the verb *diakonein* in Greek, and the one who provided service was called the *diakonos*. Jesus saw himself as a model of "one who serves." In the early church domain, debate existed regarding women's roles, just as there is debate now. Some have used this story to show that Jesus condoned this woman's service,[37] whereas others have used it to restrict women's roles to only service, which many women today regard as subservience.

By including her story, all three Synoptic Gospel writers have testified to the presence and importance of women in the early Jesus movement. They immortalized her as an early disciple and the first woman to follow Jesus. Although she displays the characteristics of a Jewish housewife, Simon Peter's mother-in-law also emulates the humble service of Jesus himself.

It is significant that the first of many physical healings that Jesus performed during his ministry involves a woman, demonstrating that women matter to Jesus and he has compassion for them.

---

[36] Ibid., Getty-Sullivan, p. 74
[37] Ibid., Getty-Sullivan p. 77

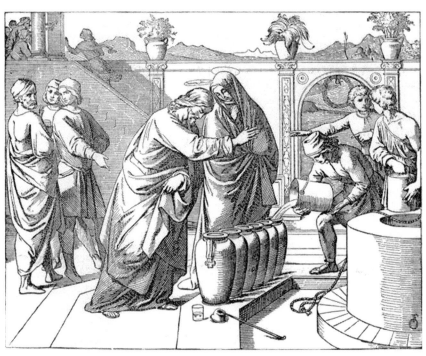

Image 5: Jesus Changes Water into Wine

CHAPTER 5:
JESUS AND HIS MOTHER
ATTEND THE CANA WEDDING

This story of the miracle at Cana *only* appears in the Gospel of John, where it is the opening event of the ministry of Jesus. In fact, 90 percent of the material in the Fourth Gospel does not appear in the other three.[38] John's account of the ministry of Jesus is quite different from their stories.[39] The fact that it was written last and relied on sources other than the Synoptic Gospels only partially explains the differences.

The author of John states clearly that he wrote the Gospel "so that you may come to believe that Jesus is the Messiah, the son of God, and that through believing, you may have life in his name."[40] John wants to show that Jesus is the fulfillment of the Jewish people's religion[41] and that he performed "signs" that revealed his powers.

John's Gospel begins with a theological prologue, which describes Jesus as "the Word that was with God in the beginning" and declares that "the Word was God."[42] That prologue is followed by a dramatic encounter with John the Baptist, who prophesied the coming of one greater than he. At Jesus's baptism, John the Baptist's testifies that he "saw the Spirit descending from heaven like a dove, and it remained on him."[43] He also

---

[38] Op. cit., Thurston, p. 78.

[39] Ibid., Thurston, p. 78.

[40] Ibid., *NRSV,* John 20:31 I am indebted to Bill Countryman, my New Testament professor and author of *The Mystical Way in the Fourth Gospel, Revised Edition* for pointing this out on page 24 of his book.

[41] Op. cit., Thurston, p. 79.

[42] Op. cit., *NRSV,* 1:1, p. 91.

[43] Ibid., *NRSV,* John 1:32, p. 92.

notes, "The one who sent me to baptize with water said to me, 'He upon whom you see the Spirit descend and remain is the one who baptizes with the Holy Spirit.' And I myself have seen and have testified this is the Son of God.[44]

After John the Baptist's testimony, two of John's disciples follow Jesus, Andrew is one of them, and he brings his brother, Simon. The next day, Jesus calls Philip, and Philip finds Nathaniel. On the following day, Jesus and his four disciples attend a wedding in Cana of Galilee, where the mother of Jesus is also present. The Gospel writer gives her title as "the mother of Jesus" to honor her for her good fortune of having a son.[45]

During the celebration, "when the wine gives out, the mother of Jesus says to him, 'They have no wine.'"[46] To run out of food or beverages would have been embarrassing to the bridal couple. Jesus replies to her, "Woman, what concern is that to you and to me? My hour has not yet come."

Mary conveys high expectations when she calls upon her son to address the shortage of wine. Implicit in her request is her sense that he has the power to produce more wine. John's Gospel suggests that mother and son share an awareness of the miraculous powers of Jesus, but this is absent from the portrayal of their relationship in the Synoptic Gospels. Jesus's initial refusal to intervene is an assertion of his freedom from Mary's parental authority. The provision of wine at a wedding banquet does not appear to be a part of the plan of Jesus when he states, "My hour has not yet come." We will never know what hour he is waiting for because he elects to avoid fighting openly with his mother. His first refusal is polite, indicating that his allegiance is to God, not his mother.

---

[44]	Ibid., *NRSV*, John 1:33b–34, p. 92.
[45]	Brown, Raymond E. *The Gospel According to John I–XII*, Garden City, Doubleday, p. 98.
[46]	Op. cit., *NRSV*, John 2:3, p. 93.

Mary ignores his refusal and directs the servants to "do whatever he tells you." Her words imply the sovereignty of Jesus, but Mary's intervention with the servants pushes Jesus to do what *she* thinks is right:

> Now standing there, were six stone water jars for the Jewish rites of purification, each holding twenty or thirty gallons. Jesus said to them, "Fill the jars with water." And they filled them up to the brim. He said to them, "Now draw some out, and take it to the chief steward." So they took it. When the steward tasted the water that had become wine, and did not know where it came from (though the servants who had drawn the water knew), the steward called the bridegroom and said to him, "Everyone serves the good wine first, and then the inferior wine. But you have kept the good wine until now."
>
> Jesus did this, the first of his signs, in Cana in Galilee, and revealed his glory; and his disciples believed in him.[47]

Comments

Although Jesus never concedes that he will accede to his mother's wishes, when the servants approach him, as they have been directed to do by her, he identifies the vessels to be filled with water. And then, miraculously, the water becomes wine. We do not see the transformation take place; we do not know what Jesus said or did to make it happen. We only know that, after the jars were filled with water, the servants obediently poured off some for the steward, which spurred the steward to declare that it was wine of a high quality. In the revised edition of the *Women's Bible Commentary*, Gail O'Day asserts that "turning water into wine is an act of turning scarcity into abundance and of reciprocal hospitality."[48] Even though he is an invited guest, Jesus chooses to give something of value back to the wedding couple by renewing the festivities with the gift of good wine.

---

[47] Op. cit., *NRSV*, John 2: 4–11, p. 93.

[48] Newsom, Ringe, and Lapsley (Eds.), *Women's Bible Commentary Revised and Updated*, p. 520.

Guided Meditation

Imagine these wedding festivities. Hear the laughter and imagine the participants" dancing and enjoying themselves.

Notice Mary there with her friends. Imagine whether she is enjoying herself.

Notice also how Mary is observing her son's movements.

Jesus is busy interacting with people, too. See how intently he engages with others. Imagine what a good time he is having.

Mary realizes that the plentiful supply of wine has dwindled. She shows concern. Imagine her thoughts.

Imagine her decision to go over to her son Jesus to tell him about the lack of wine.

Watch how his mother's pressures him. See him listening to her suggestion. Imagine what he is thinking.

Notice how Jesus shakes his head. Imagine his reaction to her and her request.

See how he politely refuses her suggestion that he do something to add to the wine supply.

Imagine Mary's reaction to her son's rebuff.

Notice that Mary does not return to her friends. Instead she is going directly to the servants. She seems to be discounting her son's refusal.

Imagine what she is instructing them to do.

Imagine those servants approaching Jesus. Does he know about his mother's intervention?

These servants create a decision point for Jesus, Will he create a domestic dispute between himself and his mother?

When Jesus speaks to the servants, he asks them to fill the empty purification jars with water. Notice how decisive he is.

Comments

A miracle takes place. The water is now a fine wine, and Mary is a crucial factor in bringing that about. Mary appears confident about Jesus's powers.

John's view of Mary depicted here contrasts with Luke's description of her opposition to Jesus's conversation with the Temple elders as a young man. Whereas Luke repeatedly depicts Mary as unaware of Jesus's messianic calling during his active ministry, John presents Mary's faith in Jesus early in his ministry, without the preparation or predictions of an angelic messenger.

I think it is more than coincidental that Jesus chooses the large jars used in the purification rituals, required by the Law of Moses, to transform the water into wine. In this way, a sign of Jesus's divine powers and God's grace replaces that Law, which is a major theme in John's Gospel. C. K.

Barrett adds, "Jesus as the fulfiller of Judaism, as the bearer of supernatural power becomes [...] an object of faith to his disciples.[49]

Reflection Questions

Have your mentors or caretakers pushed you to do more than you thought possible or appropriate? What was the result?

Have you pushed those you love to do what you think is best? What happened?

Jesus was encouraged by his mother to do the work of God. Is there someone in your life urging you to do God's work? How do you feel about doing God's work? Does it frighten you or gladden your heart?

---

[49]   C. K. Barrett, The Gospel According to St. John, 2nd Edition, p. 189

Conclusions

When I compare the three images of Jesus's mother, Mary, presented thus far—the young woman chosen by God to bear God's child, the anxious mother who finds her lost son in the Temple conversing with the elders, and the mother who wants him to miraculously produce more wine—I see aspects of a human figure with which we can all identify. They lead us to compare Mary with our own mothers or mother figures and to examine our own behavior if we have become mothers ourselves.

It is important to the themes of the Gospel of John that Mary conveys an awareness and appreciation of Jesus's mission and ministry. When John's Gospel also places Mary at the Cross, he creates a continuity to her role in Jesus's life. In contrast, the Synoptic Gospels paint a picture of Mary as a woman who is not comfortable with Jesus's ministry. Though less satisfying and perhaps even a jolt to our earliest memories of Christian teachings, I believe the earlier Synoptic accounts are more accurate; they provide us with a very believable mother and son who are at odds over how he is living his life.

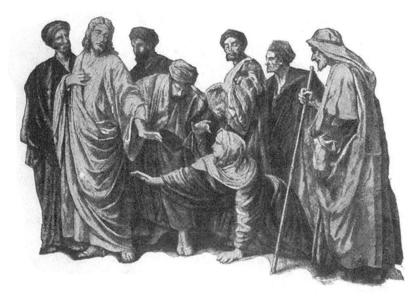

Image 6: Woman with an Issue of Blood Touches Jesus's Garment

CHAPTER 6:
JESUS HEALS A WOMAN
WITH A HEMORRHAGE

To fully understand the story of the encounter of Jesus with the woman with a hemorrhage, it is necessary to have some knowledge of ancient Judaism and its attitudes toward purity and cleanliness—especially toward women during their menstrual cycle and other periods of bleeding.

The book of Leviticus, compiled by priestly writers around 450 BC, deals with how God's covenant people were to behave in all areas of life. The purity laws defined cleanliness and uncleanness for both men and women. Holiness was dependent upon purity, and purity demanded strict obedience to the law. The laws that governed uncleanness were rigid and explicitly detailed.[50] The primary causes of uncleanness were childbirth, contact with a human corpse, the discharge of bodily fluids (especially blood), and leprosy (and other skin diseases).

Examine this background material from the Book of Leviticus 15:19–25:[51]

> When a woman has a discharge of blood that is her regular discharge from her body, she shall be in her impurity for seven days, and whoever touches her shall be unclean until the evening. Everything upon which she lies during her impurity shall be unclean; everything also upon which she sits shall be unclean. Whoever touches her bed shall wash his clothes, and bathe in

---

[50] Op. cit., Pearson, p. 98.
[51] Op. cit., *NRSV*, Leviticus 15:19–25, pp. 102–103.

water, and be unclean until evening. Whoever touches anything upon which she sits shall wash his clothes, and bathe in water, and be unclean until the evening; whether it is the bed or anything upon which she sits, when he touches it he shall be unclean until the evening. If any man lies with her, and her impurities fall on him, he shall be unclean seven days; and every bed on which he lies shall be unclean.

If a woman has a discharge of blood for many days, not at the time of her impurity, or if she has a discharge beyond the time of her impurity, all the days of her discharge she shall continue in uncleanness; as in the days of her impurity, she shall be unclean.

Women were kept separate from others whenever there was a flow of blood, whatever the cause. For the seven days of a normal menstrual cycle, a woman was kept in seclusion. A longer period of purification was required after childbirth, and it was doubled after the birth of a girl, since females were considered less clean than males.

The flow of blood isolated women and degraded them in the eyes of others. Explanations for why the purity codes had to be observed center on preserving the purity of men.[52] If this information is new to you, Anita Diamant's New York Times bestseller called *The Red Tent,* gives a vivid picture of the segregated life of women in Old Testament times. "Blood was believed to be the seat of the soul and the principal of all life"; thus, "it was extremely dangerous and taboo."[53] The laws determined "whether blood would atone and render a person holy or whether it would condemn and render a person unclean."[54]

---

[52] Op. cit., Getty-Sullivan, p. 69

[53] Op. cit., Pearson, p. 99

[54] Ibid., Pearson, p. 99

Also, according to the Law, women were in all things inferior to men. Josephus, from the first century, is quoted as saying, "Let her accordingly be submissive, not for her humiliation, but that she may be directed; for the authority has been given by God to the man."[55]

Guided Meditation

Imagine yourself living in such a society and being confined for seven out of every twenty-eight days (and more after the birth of a child).

Imagine living under laws that make you unclean and untouchable.

What effect does this have on you?

Mark's Story of a Hemorrhaging Woman

Mark tells the story of a woman who had been bleeding for twelve years. Because of her "impurity," she suffered isolation and social ostracism. If she had been married, her condition would have been grounds for divorce.

---

[55] Source unknown

51

Listen to how Mark describes the healing of this woman with a hemorrhage:

> Now there was a woman who had been suffering from hemorrhages for twelve years. She had endured much under many physicians, and had spent all that she had; and she was no better, but rather grew worse. She had heard about Jesus, and came up behind him in the crowd and touched his cloak, for she said, 'If I but touch his clothes, I will be made well.' Immediately her hemorrhage stopped; and she felt in her body that she was healed of her disease. Immediately aware that power had gone forth from him, Jesus turned about in the crowd and said, "Who touched my clothes?" And his disciples said to him, "you see the crowd pressing in on you, how can you say, 'Who touched me?'" [Jesus] looked all around to see who had done it. But the woman, knowing what had happened to her, came in fear and trembling [and] fell down before him. [Jesus] said to her, "Daughter, your faith has made you well; go in peace, and be healed of your disease." [56]

Guided Meditation

Imagine what it was like to be considered permanently unclean in Jewish culture, like the hemorrhaging woman. You would have to live an isolated existence.

Imagine not being touched, hugged, caressed or helped for twelve years.

---

[56] Op. cit., *NRSV*, Mark 5:25–34, p. 41.

You will need God's help, but you can not go and pray with the assembly in the synagogue. That is the law, but those laws are inhumane.

Imagine being unable to go where you want, because your very touch might defile others. The people in your town do not want you to go out or go to the market because they fear touching you and becoming defiled.

Imagine being that isolated and being treated like an outcast.

Imagine the frustration and despair of the hemorrhaging woman. She went to several doctors for help, and though they were quick to take her money, they were not able to cure her.

Imagine how hope arose in her when she heard about a rabbi with miraculous healing powers who had cured a woman, the mother-in-law of one of his disciples. She also heard that he was compassionate and had touched and cured a leper, an untouchable like her.

Imagine the hemorrhaging woman seeing crowds gathering around Jesus.

At first, she feels afraid to address Jesus in public. She does not want to bring attention to herself and let others realize that she is in their midst.

Imagine that she can not stop thinking that if she just touches his clothing she will get well.

Imagine how the risk makes her apprehensive.

Imagine the hemorrhaging woman moving toward Jesus.

Notice that some of the people there who know her move out of her way.

Imagine how eager she is to reach him unnoticed.

Finally, see how she pushes herself forward to touch the hem of his garment. Instantly, she feels a difference: she knows that she has been cured.

Imagine the woman's elation!

See Jesus stop suddenly and search the crowd. He asks "Who touched me?"

Imagine how scared she is becoming. She anticipates his disapproval.

She seems aware that she cannot hide from him, Imagine her kneeling in front of him, shaking with fear and admitting the truth.

Notice that Jesus does not condemn her. He proclaims to everybody that she is not unclean.

Jesus is not offended by her touch, he says her faith has cured her.

Imagine what it is like to be transformed from being a rejected woman to being loved.

Imagine her joy and thankfulness.

Reflection Questions

When have you seen yourself as one who is unclean or unacceptable? Has there been a time when you were avoided by others or not accepted and respected by them, as if you lacked dignity or worth?

Do you remember a time when you longed to be touched, to be hugged, to know that you mattered?

Are there times when you feel unacceptable today?

Do you need healing?

Try to get in touch with your own needs for healing and restoration to a full life.

Perhaps you, too, have sought help from many experts. Have you resigned yourself to your situation?

Do you believe Jesus can heal you?

Take time to identify your own needs for healing and share them here.

The story of the hemorrhaging woman reminds us that real faith involves risk. She also shows us what faith can achieve. Her life changes when she reaches out to Jesus. What risks do you need to take?

Conclusions

Jesus responded to the needs of people without regard for their cleanliness. His compassion was never limited or controlled by the purity laws. He never indicated any concern for his own cleanliness. He didn't openly object to those laws, he simply ignored them. For many in the crowd following Jesus, his acceptance of the healed woman and his response to her was shocking. By not rejecting the woman after she touched his garment, he freed her to live out the holiness that was her God-given right. The woman's risky choice that led to her healing continues to console abused women everywhere. Similarly, persons with visible disabilities have some of the same needs as the first-century woman with a hemorrhage. Consider asking your congregation what you might do to meet their needs.

It is Jesus's Good News that we are one body, a community knitted together by God's love and mercy.

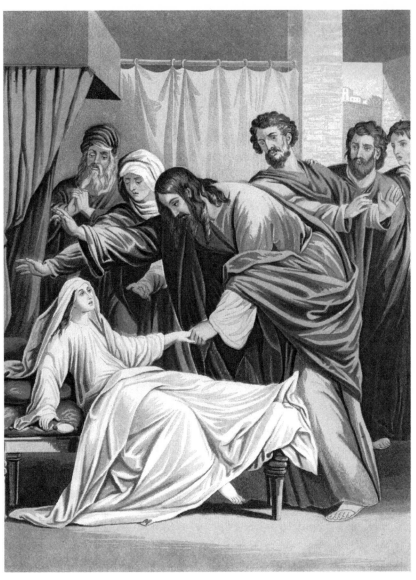

Image 7: Jesus Raising the Daughter of Jairus

CHAPTER 7:
JESUS RAISES THE DAUGHTER OF JAIRUS

As Jesus becomes known, large crowds begin to gather around him. One day, a leader of the synagogue comes to Jesus and begs him to heal his twelve-year-old daughter. He believes that Jesus is able to restore his daughter to health because he has demonstrated that he shares in God's healing powers. Jesus elects to go with the synagogue leader. However, their journey is interrupted by the incident with a woman with a hemorrhage, which is described in Chapter 6. During this time, the child dies, and the story becomes one of restoring the dead to life. Listen to how Mark describes this incident:[57]

> When Jesus had crossed again in the boat to the other side, a great crowd gathered around him; and he was by the sea. Then one of the leaders of the Synagogue named Jairus came and, when he saw him, fell at his feet and begged him repeatedly. "My little daughter is at the point of death. Come and lay your hands on her, so that she may be made well, and live." So he went with him. And a large crowd followed him and pressed in on him. (Mark 5:21–24)

> Some people came from the leader's house to say, "Your daughter is dead. Why trouble the teacher any further?" But overhearing what they said, Jesus said to the leader of the synagogue, "Do not fear, only believe." He allowed no one to follow him except Peter, James and John, the brother of James. When they came to the house of the leader of the synagogue, he saw a commotion, people

---

57 Op. cit., *NRSV*, Mark 5:21–24; 5:35–43, pp. 39–40.

weeping and wailing loudly. When he had entered, he said to them, "Why do you make a commotion and weep? The child is not dead but sleeping." And they laughed at him. Then he put them all outside, and took the child's father and mother and those who were with him, and went in where the child was. He took her by the hand and said to her "Talitha cum" which means, "Little girl, get up!" And immediately, the girl got up and began to walk about (she was twelve years of age). At this, they were overcome with amazement. [Jesus] strictly ordered them that no one should know this, and told them to give her something to eat. (Mark 5:35–43)

Comments

The signs of her restoration to life are vivid: she gets up and walks around. Jesus tells them to give her something to eat, which is another sign that she has been brought back to life. To the author of Mark, Jesus's actions demonstrate that he acts with the power of God. The command to tell no one, found throughout Mark, is designed to ensure that the revelation of Jesus's identity will only occur at the Cross. However the power of Jesus to perform miracles of this magnitude defies silence.[58]

This story also appears in the Gospels of Matthew and Luke.[59] Luke's version is almost identical to Mark's. However, in Matthew's version, Jairus is not named; the father is only described as a leader of the synagogue. He claims that his daughter has just died and he beseeches Jesus to "come and lay your hands on her and she will live." Jesus goes with him, with three of his disciples. When the crowd has been put outside, Jesus goes in and takes her by the hand. At that moment, the girl gets up. The report of this event spread throughout that district.[60]

---

[58] Op. cit., Getty-Sullivan, p. 59.
[59] Ibid., *NRSV*, Matthew 9:18–19 and 9:23–26, p. 9; Luke 8:40–56, pp. 68–69.
[60] Ibid., *NRSV* Matthew 9:25–26, p. 9.

It is one thing to cure the sick, but the view then and now is that bringing someone back from the dead is a miracle that only God can bring about. Yet, here, Jesus is shown to share in God's power to restore life. In fact, the Gospels tell us that Jesus raised three people: Jairus' only daughter, the only son of the widow from Nain (discussed in Chapter 10 of this book), and his friend Lazarus (discussed in Chapter 14). It is the father's emotional plea that elicits Jesus's concern and action. He advises him to have faith, not fear. Similarly, it is the grief expressed by the widow of Nain and the sisters of Lazarus, which occur later, that leads Jesus to resuscitate them, too.

When Jesus restores this young woman to life, he shows that he values and finds meaning in the lives of women and children as well as men. No one is insignificant in his eyes. Each person is worth his attention.

A twelve-year-old girl was eligible for marriage at that time. In that patriarchal culture, this involved a transition from her father's house to the house of her husband. It was also the time when her body transitioned from childhood to womanhood. Some scholars think that her age is cited because Jairus' sorrow would have been greater if she had died at that age because his daughter had just reached the normal age for marriage and would likely fetch him a bride price and grandchildren.

Notice that the girl is only known as Jairus' daughter. Mary Ann Getty-Sullivan attributes this to the custom that "a girl only acquires a name of her own when she has a son, until then she is identified as related to some other man, first her father and later her husband."[61] While this sounds plausible (because it fits in with the lower status of women then), I have found no other scholar who makes this same claim.

---

[61]   Op. cit., Getty-Sullivan, p. 55.

Guided Meditation

Consider the stress being experienced by this family. Imagine their sense of urgency because their child is suffering.

Imagine the discussion that sent Jairus racing off to find Jesus.

Imagine the sick young woman, lying lifeless at home with her mother while Jairus, her father, seeks help from Jesus. See how her condition weakens minute by minute.

Imagine the young girl's fear that she may die before Jesus reaches her.

See how the girl weakens. Imagine her, as she reviews the important moments in her life.

Imagine the prayers she expresses that Jesus will save her.

Imagine her reaction when Jesus brings her back to life.

Reflection Questions for Women

Jairus' daughter had begun puberty. Think back to the time when you began menstruating and developing breasts. How did you feel about the changes that were happening in you?

Did anyone else recognize the emergence of those changes? How did they react?

What came up for you during these reflections?

Conclusions

This story conveys the compassion of Jesus, first for the desperation of the young girl's father, and then for his mortally ill daughter. Once he promises to help, he is not dissuaded by the news that she has died; instead, he asks the father to believe in his powers. When he enters their home, he scorns the mourners and sends them away. Though they don't believe him, when he tells them the girl is just sleeping, they go as he instructs them.

When Jesus comes into the presence of the dead young girl, he touches her without hesitation and calls upon her to get up. His tone is confidant, his instructions to the girl and her parents clear. When she rises and walks around, it is a sure sign that she is alive, and the disciples are witnesses to his divine power.

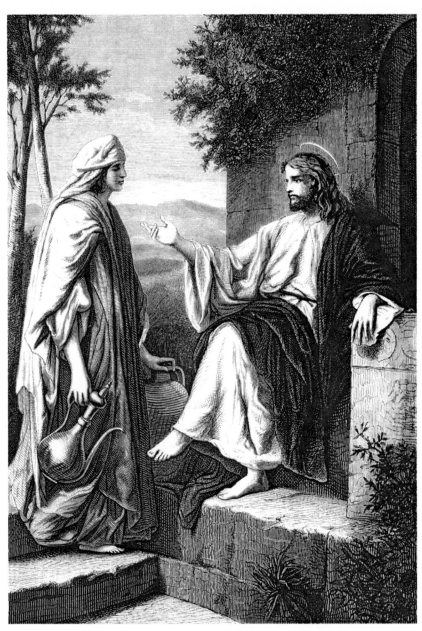

Image 8: Jesus Speaks to a Samaritan Woman

CHAPTER 8:
JESUS MEETS A SAMARITAN
WOMAN AT THE WELL

Jesus takes respite by the well of Jacob in Samaria at high noon. It is very hot. He is on his way back to Galilee from Judea. Meanwhile, his disciples go off to purchase food in the nearby town of Sychar. An unaccompanied Samaritan woman comes to fetch water, despite the heat. Ordinarily, women would come in groups to gather water—either in the early morning or at dusk. Thus, her behavior is unusual. Jesus initiates a conversation with her, even though he does not know her and Jews did not associate with Samaritans. In fact, Jews and Samaritans despised and distrusted one another. The woman is surprised when Jesus speaks to her, and when his disciples later find him engaged in conversation with her, they too are surprised. Most Jews preferred to travel out of their way in order to bypass Samaria on their way to or from Jerusalem.

The hostility between the Jews and Samaritans was a long-standing animosity. The Samaritans traced their history to their ancestors, Abraham, Isaac, and Jacob, and they treasured the shrines where they had encountered God and worshiped. The only scripture they accepted was the Torah, the first five books of Moses. Samaria was the capital of the Northern Kingdom before it was sacked by the Assyrians in 721 BC. At that time, the Samaritans were taken into captivity. When the Samaritans returned from exile, they were shunned by the Jews because they had intermarried with their Assyrian conquerors and worshipped at Mt. Gerizim (not Jerusalem). In short, they were deemed unclean. Their land was situated between the Jews in Galilee to the north, where the towns of Nazareth, Capernaum, Cana, and Tiberias were located, and the Jews in the south, who were devoted to the monarchies of Saul, David, and Solomon and worshiped at the Temple in Jerusalem.

Reflection Questions

Are there groups of people that you have been taught to hate or distrust? Who are the Samaritans in your life?

Have you ever been ostracized or made to feel inferior or unwelcome, like the Samaritans? How did you (or do you now) deal with being labeled and excluded?

The Conversation between Jesus and the Samaritan Woman

Read John's story of Jesus's encounter with the Samaritan woman at Jacob's well:

> [Jesus] left Judea and started back to Galilee. But he had to go through Samaria. So he came to a Samaritan city called Sychar, near the plot of ground that Jacob had given to his son Joseph. Jacob's well was there and Jesus, tired out by his journey, was sitting by the well. It was about noon.

Women Who Knew Jesus

A Samaritan woman came to draw water, and Jesus said to her, "Give me a drink." (His disciples had gone to the city to buy food.) The Samaritan woman said to him, "How is it that you, a Jew, ask a drink of me, a woman of Samaria?" (Jews do not share things in common with Samaritans).[62]

Jesus initiates this conversation, but notice how unreceptive she is to his request. She cannot imagine why a Jew would seek water from a Samaritan water jar. Samaritan women did not practice the Jewish purity codes, so "one could never be certain if a Samaritan woman was not in a state of uncleanness," which would affect the vessel she carried.[63] No decent Jewish man would have spoken to her or risked contamination by drinking from her water jar. Thus, Jesus breaks two significant boundaries in his conversation with the Samaritan woman: "the boundary between male and female and the boundary between the chosen people and people they rejected [like the Samaritans.]"[64]

Guided Meditation

Place yourself in this story. Imagine yourself in the Samaritan town of Sychar, in central Palestine on a very hot day.

You are a woman wanting to draw water at this time in order to avoid the other townspeople. You do not wish to be humiliated, but you need water to survive.

---

[62] Op. cit., NRSV, John 4:3–9, pp. 94–95.

[63] Barrett, C. K., p. 23.

[64] Op cit, Newsom, Ringe, and Lapse (Eds.), p. 521.

71

Your ancestors also drew from this same well, so you cherish this place.

You pause as you approach the well and look out over the broad, fertile plains surrounding your town.

As you feel the heat of the noonday sun on your face, you envy the townspeople who can avoid this heat by resting in their homes or sitting in the shade.

You set your water jug down at the well and notice a stranger seated there.

Before you can flee, he speaks to you and says courteously, "Give me a drink." Imagine your reaction.

You hesitate. Men are not supposed to speak to women they do not know. This man appears to be from Galilee, and there is much hostility between your people and his. Imagine reacting to his request.

The Conversation Continues

> Jesus answered her, "If you knew the gift of God, and who it is that is saying to you, 'Give me a drink,' you would have asked him, and he would have given you living water."[65] The woman said to him, "Sir, you have no bucket, and the well is deep. Where do you get that living water? Are you greater than our ancestor Jacob, who gave us this well, and with his sons and his flocks drank from it?" Jesus said to her, "Everyone who drinks of *this* water will be thirsty again, but those who drink of the water I will give them, will never be thirsty. The water that I will give will become in them a spring of water gushing up to eternal life." The woman said to him, "Sir, give me this water, so that I may never be thirsty or have to keep coming here to draw water."[66]

The unnamed Samaritan Woman shares an important trait with Jesus that is not spoken aloud: they are both outcasts. She hears the freedom being offered by Jesus. With his water, she will never be thirsty and will never again have to seek water when it's hot and there is the potential of being snubbed or scorned.

Living water suggests a running stream (in contrast to well water); Jesus is promising a resource that brings everlasting life.

---

[65] Op. cit., *NRSV*, John 4:10–15, p. 95. "Life-giving water appears in several important passages in John 3:5; 4:10–15; 7:38; 19:34. The "water" is preeminently the Holy Spirit, which alone gives life."

[66]

Reflection Questions

Imagine Jesus telling you that if you know who he is, you will not hesitate. He says you will ask him for living water. How does his promise affect you? What hopes and longings do his words evoke?

Jesus speaks of her thirst. Are you thirsty? Thirsty for what?

Are you in need of the living water that Jesus is offering?

The Conversation Continues

Immediately following that short exchange, we read the following:

> Jesus said to her, "Go call your husband, and come
> back." The woman answered him, "I have no husband."
> Jesus said to her, "You are right in saying, 'I have no
> husband;' for you have had five husbands, and the one
> you have now is not your husband! What you have said
> is true!"[67]

Jesus tells the woman the truth about herself, but there is no judgment or criticism. Here, the woman's real social status is revealed. Not only is she a Samaritan, she has been married five times and is now living with yet another man to whom she is not married. The reasons for her marital history do not seem to concern Jesus, nor does he pass moral judgment on her. Instead, he confirms that she has told the truth! The conversation about the woman's husbands shows Jesus's ability to see and know all things, which causes the woman to see Jesus differently.[68] And she responds to Jesus with the words, "Sir, I see that you are a prophet."[69]

Guided Meditation

Imagine the Samaritan woman's reactions to such intimate knowledge and revelations about herself.

---

67 Ibid., <u>NRSV</u>, John 4:16-18, p. 95

68 Op Cit., <u>Newsom</u>, Ringe & Lapsley, p. 522

69 Op. cit., <u>NRSV</u>, John 4: 19b, p. 95

She recalls the hope for the arrival of God's Promised One and tells him, "I know the Messiah is coming." Jesus replies, "I am he." Imagine her response to those words.

The Conversation Continues

Her recognition of Jesus as a prophet leads her to ask him the most pressing religious question that divides the Jews and the Samaritans. She is the first woman to engage Jesus in a significant theological discussion, and she does so by saying the following:

> "Our ancestors worshipped on this mountain, but you say that the place where people must worship is in Jerusalem." Jesus said to her, "Woman, believe me, the hour is coming when you will worship [God] neither on this mountain nor in Jerusalem. You worship what you do not know; we worship what we know, for salvation is from the Jews. But the hour is coming, and is now here, when the true worshipers will worship [God] in spirit and truth, for [God] seeks such as these to worship [God]. God **is** spirit and those who worship [God] must worship in spirit and truth."

In saying this, Jesus does away with regionalism, as shown in the rivalry between the Samaritan's Mt. Gerizim and the Jews' Jerusalem and Mt. Zion. He envisions worship occurring everywhere with people worshiping God in spirit and truth. These new religious truths exclaimed by Jesus are much clearer in Peterson's translation[70]:

> Jesus answered, "believe me woman, the time is coming when you Samaritans will worship God neither here at this mountain nor there in Jerusalem. You worship guessing in the dark; we Jews worship in the clear light of day. God's way of salvation is made available through the Jews. But the time is coming – it has, in fact, come – when what you're called will not matter and where you go to worship will not matter. It's who you are and the way you live that count before God. Your worship must engage your spirit in the pursuit of truth. That's the kind of people God is out looking for: those who are simply and honestly themselves before God in their worship. God is sheer being itself – Spirit. Those who worship God must do it out of their very being, their spirits, their true selves, in adoration."

Jesus claims that wherever we worship, the place becomes holy and sacred because it is there we meet God.[71] We can be anywhere. The sparring between Jesus and the Samaritan woman becomes a profound teaching: God is looking for "those who are simply and honestly themselves before God in their worship."[72] Thus, worship can happen anywhere because God meets us wherever we are if we come with an open heart. A full understanding of this teaching could result in changing the tradition-bound liturgical practices of many denominations.

---

[70] Op. cit., *MSG*, John 4:21–24, pp. 1331–1332.

[71] Op. cit., Pearson, p. 148.

[72] Op. cit., *MSG*, John 4:23b, p. 1932.

Reflection Question

Are you simply and honestly yourself before God in your worship?

How might Jesus's comments change your worship practices and prayer life?

The Conversation Continues

According to Jesus, it no longer matters whether you are a Jew or a Samaritan; what matters is the kind of person you are and the way you live your life. Where you worship no longer matters; what matters is the wholehearted way you respond to God.

Suddenly, the woman's faith expands and she says the following to him:

> "I do know that Messiah is coming" (who is called Christ). "When he comes, he will proclaim all things to

us." Jesus said to her, "I am he, the one who is speaking to you."[73]

For the first time in the Gospel of John, Jesus reveals himself to be the Messiah; the Samaritan woman is given the truth of who he is. He uses the *I am* self-designation that characterizes John's Christology. For John, "Jesus is the way, the truth and the life!" Notice that it is not to his close disciples that he reveals his messianic calling; his ultimate truth is given to this nameless woman.

> Just then his disciples came. They were astonished that he was speaking with a woman, but no one said, "what do you want?" or "Why are you speaking with her?" Then the woman left her water jar and went back to the city. She said to the people, "Come and see a man who told me everything I have ever done! He cannot be the Messiah, can he?" They left the city and were on their way to him.[74]

Guided Meditation

Imagine the Samaritan woman suddenly hearing voices and turning to see several men approaching. They seem surprised to find their companion talking to her, but they say nothing. Notice their faces as they look at her and back at him.

---

[73] Op. cit., *NRSV,* John 4: 25–26, p. 95.
[74] Op. cit., *NRSV,* John 4: 27-30, p. 95

Excited by what has transpired with this stranger, she sets down her water jar and rushes back to the town to tell people about this man who really knew her and promised her life-giving water. Imagine her feelings as she shares her good news with the very people she usually avoids.

Comments

Free of her shame, the Samaritan woman proclaims the identity of the man who spoke directly to her. She witnesses to the spirit and truth of the revelation of Jesus and evangelizes the Samaritans, not because she was asked or authorized to do so, but because her faith in her experience with Jesus compels her to. Her encounter with Jesus changes her. No longer a self-perceived outcast who is shunned by others, she becomes a witness heard by her townspeople and through whom they come to believe in Jesus. In John's Gospel, one who witnesses to Jesus (i.e., sees him and tells others about that experience) has the mark of discipleship.

Reflection Questions

When you meet Jesus or encounter God, it is hard to remain silent. Have your experiences with God ever compelled you to speak up?

Do you connect with the Samaritan woman for this reason? Write about it here.

The End of the Story

The story closes in the following manner:

> So when the Samaritans came to Jesus, they asked him to stay with them; and he stayed there two days. And many more believed because of his word. They said to the woman, "It is no longer because of what you said that we believe for we have heard for ourselves, and we know that that this is truly the Savior of the world."[75]

The Samaritan woman is remembered in this Gospel because her experience of Jesus leads her to believe and tell others that they might see for themselves and believe as well. Do not miss the irony that Jesus is rejected by the Jews and accepted by the Samaritans. The once-scorned Samaritan woman becomes an evangelist who is accepted by both groups. She reminds us that, in God's realm, there are no outcasts or second-class citizens.[76] Jesus came so that we all might believe and have life in him. Through Jesus, "all barriers of tradition, race, nationality, gender and prejudice were transcended."[77]

---

[75]   Op. cit., *NRSV,* John 4: 40-42, p. 95

[76]   A phrase made popular during the 1980's by the Most Right Rev. Edmund Browning, as Presiding Bishop of the Episcopal Church of the USA.

[77]   Op cit, Pearson, p. 154

Reflection Questions

Think about your own life. If you were to encounter Jesus today, what hidden truth would Jesus know about that would make you feel truly known and accepted?

The Samaritan woman at the well had an empty jug to offer Jesus. If you think of yourself as an empty earthen vessel, what can you offer to Jesus at this time?

If Jesus knew her secrets, this story suggests that he knows yours. What part of yourself needs to be known and accepted by Jesus? Does that make you feel vulnerable or accepted for who you really are? (You may wish to place your answer on a separate piece of paper.)

Notice how frank and direct Jesus is. How does that affect you?

What started as a seemingly chance and unsolicited conversation resulted in this woman's conversion. Her excitement about Jesus leads her to leave her water jar and boldly tell others about him. How might this event apply to our efforts to evangelize today?

Conclusions

The story of the Samaritan woman is another sign of Jesus's acceptance of those whom society rejects; it created the path for the proclamation of the gospel to all peoples. The Samaritan woman is remembered because she was changed from an outcast shunned by others to a witness whom others heard and through whom others believed.[78] Her experience with Jesus corresponds to the story Jesus tells when asked to define "Who is my neighbor?" according to the commandment to love.

---

[78]   Op. cit. Getty-Sullivan, p. 94

Jesus explains that a man is left for dead on the highway after being seriously injured by thieves; others pass by without helping because touching a corpse would make them unclean. It is a man from Samaria who rescues him and ensures his full recovery. He is forever remembered as the Good Samaritan.

The Samaritan woman's experience is a reminder to all of us that Jesus offers us a role in telling others the Good News and spreading the joy to be found in a life in Christ.

In this story, we see that Jesus's gifts to humanity are many. One revealed here is acceptance; another is emancipation and freedom; and a third is a profound knowledge that is all-knowing. This is what he offers to the woman from Samaria and to us. In Luke 4:18 Jesus quoted Isaiah and said the following of himself:

> "The Spirit of the Lord is upon me, because God has anointed me to bring good news to the poor. God has sent me to proclaim release to the captives and recovery of sight to the blind, to let the oppressed go free."[79]

We are the poor and the captives. The poverty of our lives is created by our limited resources and our restricted vision; we are captives to the world's values and mores that derive from status, power, and wealth, and we are blind to what we are missing that may be found in God. This woman is changed after her discussion with Jesus; her guilt is transformed into a new life of freedom, especially freedom from guilt. The same message is repeated in John 8:31 when Jesus says the following:

> "If you continue in my word, you are truly my disciples; and you will know the truth and the truth will set you free."

---

[79] Op. cit., *NRSV*, Luke 4:18, p. 61.

This story displays many of Jesus's human traits: he is tired and thirsty, which prompts him to stop at the well. He is forthright and nonjudgmental. Once he engages in a conversation with the woman, he takes her seriously. We are given a glimpse of his God-like love, which is like a "spring of water gushing up to life "everlasting." Soon, the woman's perception of Jesus shifts from that of a Jewish man in hostile territory to seeing him as the long-awaited Messiah. Her testimony got many others to know Jesus and believe in him. She is the first female evangelist to people outside the house of Israel.

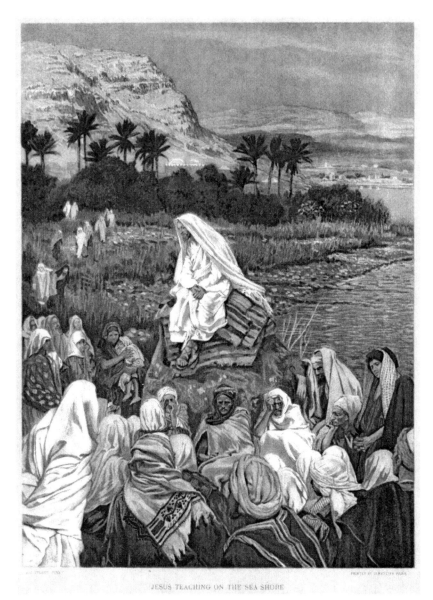

JESUS TEACHING ON THE SEA SHORE

Image 9: Jesus Teaching at the Seashore

CHAPTER 9: JESUS DISMISSES HIS MOTHER

In Mark's Gospel, the question—who is Jesus—is raised repeatedly, but in that Gospel, Jesus makes few claims about himself. When others recognize him, he tells them to tell no one. In this passage, the two groups that should have recognized him were his mother and the scribes who taught the Law, but Lamar Williamson, among others, claims that they "are both blind to his true identity."[80]

All three Synoptic Gospels present a brief incident that shows a rift between Jesus and his mother and her children. This event occurs when Jesus is teaching a large crowd in an enclosed space, which is too crowded for her to gain entry. Because I was unable to find an illustration of Jesus teaching in an enclosed space, I have substituted Image 9, which shows Jesus teaching outside. You will have to use your imagination to fully appreciate the scene.

In Mark's version of this story, Jesus's mother expresses "concern for him," but her concern may really be "a concern for the reputation of her own family."[81] She appears to believe he is insane. They have gone to where he is preaching, and they are intent on taking him away.

Listen to how Mark sees Jesus's response to his mother and her children:

> [Jesus] went home; and the crowd came together again, so that they could not even eat. When his family heard it, they went out to restrain him, for people were saying, "He has gone out of his mind." And the scribes

---

[80]

[81] Williamson, Lamar, *Mark: Interpretation: A Bible Commentary for Teaching and Preaching*, 1983, p.83.

who came down from Jerusalem said, "He has Beelzebul[82] and by the ruler of the demons he casts out demons."[83]

Then his mother and his brothers came; and standing outside, they sent to him and called him. A crowd was sitting around him; and they said to him, "Your mother and your brothers and sisters are outside, asking for you." And [Jesus] replied, "Who are my mother and my brothers?" And looking at those who sat around him, he said. "Here are my mother and brothers! Whoever does the will of God is my brother and sister and mother."[84]

Guided Meditation

Jesus's mother appears to believe that he is insane. The verb used literally means "to stand outside of," an image reflected by the idiom "to be beside oneself" or "to be eccentric," but it is rightly rendered by the following idioms: 'he is out of his mind' or 'he's gone mad.'[85] Imagine her consternation when her neighbors question her about Jesus.

Imagine this mother, who conforms to the social expectations of women, wrestling with the realization that her son's lifestyle and concerns are unlike hers and those of the men she respects in her community.

---

[82]   According to *Harper's Biblical Dictionary,* 1985, *Beelzebul,* also spelled *Baalzebub,* was a god worshipped by the Philistines, mentioned in 2 Kings 1: 2–16. In the intertestamental period, this was one of the names used to designate the forces of evil. Jesus refers to Beelzebul as the "prince of demons."

[83]   Op. cit., *NRSV,* Mark 3:19b–22, p. 37.

[84]   Ibid., *NRSV,* Mark 3:31–35, pp. 37–38.

[85]   69, Op. cit., Williamson, pp. 83-84.

Jesus says his life is centered on doing God's will. Imagine her realization that his understanding of God is leading him away from accepted Jewish practice, arousing the objections of the religious authorities.

Comments

Because our contemporary culture emphasizes the realization of our own ambitions and willful control of our own lives and success—even at the expense of others—we may find the objections of Jesus's Jewish family to be difficult to understand. Conversely, there may be many today who are like the family of Jesus because they also find Jesus's God-centered values unrealistic and unappealing.

Jesus says that those who matter to him are those who hear him, understand him, and follow the will of God as he does. This is much more than just belief *in* Jesus. How we live our lives is what matters to him, *not* the certainty of our faith *or* our status or education or wealth.

Reflection Questions

Do you try to center your life on doing God's will?

How do you ascertain God's will?

Do God's ways sometimes seem unattainable or undesirable?

Comments

A similar exchange with Jesus's family appears in Matthew 12:46–50 and Luke 8:19–21. Matthew refers to those listening to Jesus as his disciples (here, I'm using a lowercase *d* because I'm referring to pupils of a teacher or followers), and Jesus says *they* are his mother and brothers because "whoever does the will of God *is* my brother and sister and mother."

In Luke's Gospel, Jesus is told, "your mother and brothers are standing outside, wanting to see you." But Jesus answers, "My mother and my brothers are those who hear the word of God and do it."

In his translation of all three Gospels, Peterson adds a visual clarification that is poignant. His Jesus says, "Obedience is thicker than blood. The person who obeys God's will is my brother and sister and mother." Jesus's pronouncements about family recognizes that there are times when families are at odds with God.

None of these accounts, however, provide any indication that Jesus's family listened to him … yet they were in the vicinity and could have listened.

Jesus invites each of us to join his new family and center our lives in God. This is a liberating process because we become freed to be our truest selves. However, like Jesus, we may become alienated from our own families of origin if we do that. By stepping out into the light of God's realm, our families may be unwilling or unable to go there, too.

This was my experience when I first converted to Christianity. Even thirty years later, when I finally consented to seek ordination, I feared that I would be disowned. However, to my surprise, coming out from the shadows of being a closet Christian allowed my mother to get to know and accept me.

Reflection Questions

Has your faith in Jesus had its cost in disrupted family relations? What have you gained? What have you lost?

Through baptism, we are adopted into God's family. Feel the fullness now of your adoption and write about it here.

Jesus is clear: intimacy with God and the pursuit of God's goals is more important than family. If you have been raised to give family priority, does this raise issues for you?

By refusing to comply with his family, Jesus sets himself apart. And by aligning himself with those who are faithful to God, he enters into a new, intimate community that replaces his family. Where do you find community? Who or what sustains you on your spiritual journey?

Conclusions

Jesus resisted the patriarchal bonds of family obligations on many occasions. He did so whenever those ties interfered with his compliance with and devotion to the will of God. Some of those passages are reprinted below.

Mark 10:28–30

> Peter began to say to him, "Look, we have left everything and followed you." Jesus said, "Truly I tell you, there is no one who has left house or brothers and sisters or mother or father or children or fields, for my sake and for the sake of the Good News, who will not receive a hundredfold now in this age [...] and in the age to come eternal life."

> "Do not think I have come to bring peace on earth; I have not come to bring peace, but a sword. For I have come to set a man against his father, and a daughter against her mother, and a daughter-in-law against her mother-in-law; and one's foes will be members of one's own household."[86]

Matthew 10:37

> "Whoever loves father or mother more than me is not worthy of me; and whoever loves son or daughter more than me is not worthy of me."[87]

Matthew 19:29

---

[86] Op. cit., *NRSV* Mark 10:28–30, p. 46.
[87] Op. cit., *NRSV*, Matthew 10:37, p. 11.

"And everyone who has left houses or brothers or sisters or father or mother or children or fields, for my name's sake, will receive a hundredfold, and will inherit eternal life."[88]

Luke 14:26

"Whoever comes to me and does not hate father, mother, wife and children, brothers and sisters, yes, even life itself, cannot be my disciple."[89]

These statements demonstrate that personal and spiritual bonds to Jesus and God are far more important to Jesus than the bonds of family. Compared to his own family, Jesus appears to be marching to the beat of a different drummer—his central concerns and lifestyle are so unlike theirs. His life is centered on doing God's will, rather than family conformity. He is also at odds with the religious authorities who claim he is under the influence of demons because he is preaching a new understanding of God and an ethic of social justice.

---

[88]   Ibid., *NRSV*, Matthew 19:29, p. 21.
[89]   Ibid., *NRSV*, Luke 14:2, p. 77.

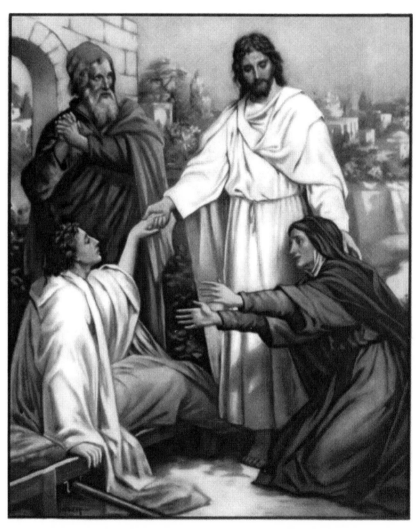

Image 10: Jesus Raises the Widow of Nain's Son

CHAPTER 10:
JESUS RAISES THE SON
OF THE WIDOW FROM NAIN

Luke's Gospel tells a story about Jesus's encounter with a widow who is grieving the loss of her only child. And because a childless widow is without resources or support, she is likely to be destitute. In that culture, a woman had almost no legal or economic standing except through a man—father, husband, son, or brother. But because this woman outlived the males in her life, she is need of God's help.

Jesus arrives at a village called Nain. A large crowd and his disciples accompany him. Luke reports:

> As he approached the gate of the town, a man who had died was being carried out. He was his mother's only son, and she was a widow; and with her was a large crowd from the town. When [Jesus] saw her, he had compassion for her and said to her, "Do not weep." Then he came forward and touched the bier, and the bearers stood still. And he said, "Young man, I say to you: rise!" The dead man sat up and began to speak, and Jesus gave him to his mother. Fear seized all of them; and they glorified God, saying "A great prophet has risen among us!" and "God has looked favorably on [God's] people!" The word about him spread throughout Judea and all the surrounding country.[90]

Comments

The details in this account correspond to what we know of the burial practices in Palestine during the first century: the use of a stretcher that Luke calls a *bier,* which is a Greek term; the funeral procession of bier bearers and mourners; and the burial outside city walls. The stretcher protects those carrying it from exposure to the corpse, which would make them unclean. The burial grounds are outside the city for the same reason: to keep the citizens clean within the city limits. Burial is the final step of the process of dying. It means that the person's life is over, that all hope is lost.

The large crowd attending the burial is evidence of their sympathy for the widow's situation. Yet she seems very alone in her sorrow and despair. Fortunately for her, Jesus is compassionate. His movement is stopped by the funeral procession, and he focuses on the widow and her grief for her dead son. Jesus is moved by her sorrow, and he performs a miracle without being asked because he feels such pity for the woman. His actions show us a God who cares.

Reflection Questions

There is a great deal of sadness whenever children have to bury a parent. If this has occurred in your life, take time to remember the experience of burying your parent or parents.

But the loss of a parent does not compare with the grief that arises when parents bury their children. If you know about this loss or have experienced it, write about it here.

Guided Meditation

Imagine this widow standing apart from the crowd as her son's bier passes through the town of Nain.

Feel the depth of her sorrow. She has lost both her spouse and her only child – and with those deaths, all sources of support and protection.

Consider how alone she seems despite the crowds that are present.

Imagine the weight of her grief because her life's purposes and joy have been taken from her.

After his journey, Jesus comes upon this scene. He sees the funeral procession carrying the deceased young man. Imagine his compassion as he eyes the grief-stricken mother of the boy, who is already a widow.

Imagine how moved Jesus is as he approaches the bier and touches it, despite the purity codes that prohibit touching anything that touches a corpse.

Imagine how eager Jesus is to return the son to his mother

Notice that as Jesus speaks, the young man sits up and speaks. He to showing everyone that he is alive.

Imagine how awed the crowd becomes. There is a hushed silenced.

Imagine the widow's response as her only son is brought to life again.

Comments

Jesus's actions are very simple and straightforward. He is touched by the mother's sorrow and united with her in empathy. Although she makes no request of him, he takes the initiative: he touches the bier, speaks, and brings the young man back to life. Everyone present sees that the son is alive and knows that a powerful change has taken place.

We are not told about the mother's reaction to her son's resuscitation, but consider the crowd's response. They speak together like a chorus, giving voice to the faith and praise generated by Jesus raising a person from the dead. Eugene Peterson describes it in *The Message*[91] as follows:

> They all realized they were in a place of holy mystery, that God was at work among them. They were quietly worshipful – and then noisily grateful, calling out among themselves, "God is back looking to the needs of the people."

In Israel, a prophet spoke for God; by word and action, a prophet brought the word of God to impact the lives of the people. For Luke, this is an act of God's grace. It prefaces Luke's later statement in Jesus's message to John the Baptist: "The dead are raised up." Jesus's fame spreads as a result of this miracle. Luke tells us this story to evoke our reaction, too.

Conclusions

Think about this story. Haven't two people been given back their lives, both the mother and her son? Not only is the son restored to his widowed mother, but he restores her place in the social order.[92]

This story corresponds closely with the stories in the Hebrew Bible, of the prophets Elijah and Elisha, who both restored life to young men.

---

[91] Op. cit., *MSG* p. 1879.
[92] Op. cit., Thurston, p. 104.

Luke adds other parallels: both mothers are widows; both prophets meet her at a city gate; after his life was restored, both prophets "gave him to his mother." Getty-Sullivan points out a significant difference between these stories: Elijah had to stretch himself over the boy three times, but Jesus raises the widow's son with a single oral command.[93] After incidents like this one, Jesus began to be regarded as a far greater prophet than Elijah, who had raised from the dead the son of the widow of Zarephath.

Jesus's concern for the poor and oppressed is well documented. Leonard Swidler reminds us that women were often the ones who suffered most, and widows were the most oppressed of all women.[94] Of the eight stories about widows in the Gospels, seven of them appear in the Gospel of Luke. In the early Christian communities, widows received charitable assistance.

Widows' circumstances vary greatly today due to variations in their status based on the culture in which they exist and the extent of preparation and planning that takes place before they become widows. There are now different classes of people who are equivalent to the destitute widows of the past. Jesus cares about their circumstances, too, and he urges us to be concerned with their care.

---

[93] Op. cit., Getty-Sullivan, p. 49.

[94] Op. cit., Swidler, p. 64.

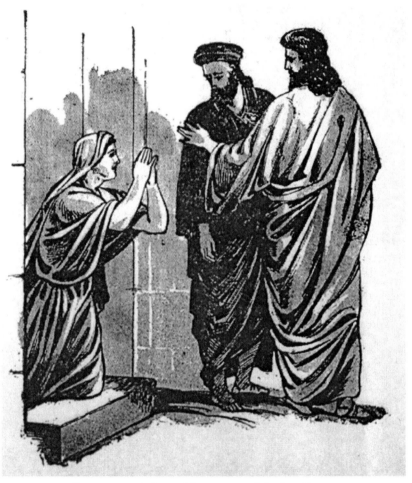

**Image 11: A Syro-Phoenician Mother Begs
Jesus to Heal Her Daughter**

CHAPTER 11:
A SYRO-PHOENICIAN WOMAN
CHALLENGES JESUS

Seeking respite, Jesus leaves Judea and travels to the Greek seaport city of Tyre, which was also a part of the Roman Empire. From accounts in the Hebrew Bible, we know that the Jews regarded Tyre as a symbol of wealth and idol worship, stemming from the fact that Ahab's wife came from Tyre. When she married Ahab, she brought her devotion to the god Baal with her and offended Elijah the prophet. The Jews referred to those non-Jewish people as Greeks. Other synonyms for Gentiles at that time were *pagans*, *sinners*, and even *dogs*.

The reputation of Jesus precedes his arrival. A desperate mother is told about his healing powers and his unexpected visit to that city. She rushes to meet him and pleads insistently.

> [Jesus] entered a house and did not want anyone to know he was there. Yet he could not escape notice. A woman whose little daughter had an unclean spirit immediately heard about him, and she came and bowed down at his feet. Now the woman was a Gentile, of Syro-Phoenician origin. She begged [Jesus] to cast the demon out of her daughter. He said to her, "Let the children be fed first, for it is not fair to take the children's food and throw it to the dogs." But she answered him, "Sir, even the dogs under the table eat the children's crumbs." Then he said to her, "For saying that, you may go – the demon has left your daughter." So she went home, found the child lying on the bed, and the demon gone.[95]

---

[95] Op. cit., *NRSV,* Mark 7:24–30, p. 42.

Comments

Jesus's initial curtness toward this woman is astonishing. Although he is known widely for his affirmative attitude toward women and sensitivity to those in need, he is disrespectful and antagonistic in this instance. In essence, he says, "I'm here for the Jews, not you pagans! You are dogs! Go away!" His language and his reaction can only be explained by the centuries of animosity between the peoples of that region as well as the fact that her intrusion is unwelcome.

Jesus surely met his match with this intrusive and insistent Greek mother. She is not dissuaded by his lack of courtesy or his insult. She knows that she has no claim on Jesus,[96] but she is on a mission to save her daughter, which is of such importance and urgency that she ignores his rebuff and the custom that women do not approach men. She realizes that there may not be another opportunity to get the attention and assistance of Jesus.

With a quick and sassy retort that surprises even Jesus, Peterson gives her the following reply in Mark's account in *The Message*:

"Of course, Master. But don't dogs under the table get scraps dropped by the children?"[97]

Refusing to be intimidated, she challenges the prevailing tradition and laws regarding the privileged role of God's "chosen people." Jesus likes her strong faith and gives in; he allows himself to be influenced by a woman!

---

[96] Op. cit., Pearson, p. 80.
[97] Op. cit., *MSG*, p. 1838

Reflection Questions

Many of us have had experiences where our love for our children, our spouse, or ourselves is so strong that we become uncharacteristically insistent. Has this happened to you?

What was at stake that led you to act?

Did anything occur that led you to back down?

Were you successful?

Is there any likelihood that you would act that way again?

Comments

This event marks the broadening of Jesus's own vision of the parameters of his ministry. He shifts away from the separatist traditions of the Hebrew culture to a more inclusive attitude. As a result, this story provided guidance to the young Christian communities regarding their treatment of non-Christians and authorized their mission to the Gentiles.

The version of this story in Matthew is better known because the Revised Common Lectionary has selected Matthew's embellishment of the story for use in Sunday worship. Matthew's woman dares to raise her voice and cry out, and this heightens the intensity of the dialogue. Note the significant ways that Matthew alters the story[98]:

---

[98]   Frances Taylor Gench, <u>Back to the Well, Women's Encounters with Jesus in the</u> Gospels, p. 1

Jesus left that place and went away to the district of Tyre and Sidon. Just then a Canaanite woman from that region came out and started shouting, "Have mercy on me, Lord, son of David, my daughter is tormented by a demon." But he did not answer her at all. And his disciples came and urged him, saying, "Send her away, for she keeps shouting after us." [Jesus] answered, "I was sent only to the house of Israel." But she came and knelt before him, saying "Lord help me." [Jesus] answered "It is not fair to take the children's food and throw it to the dogs." She said, "Yes, Lord, yet even the dogs eat the crumbs that fall from their masters' table." Then Jesus answered her, "Woman, great is your faith. Let it be done as you wish." And her daughter was healed instantly.[99]

A strong emphasis of Matthew's story is the behavior of the non-Jewish woman. She is alone in public, which is contrary to the customs imposed on Jewish women. She acts in an unfeminine fashion by raising her voice and crying out.[100] Her behavior is very different than the woman with a hemorrhage who only reached out to touch the hem of Jesus's garment and said nothing to avoid notice. This non-Jewish woman appears totally unconcerned with how she is perceived or treated, unlike most women of that time. Jesus's initial unwillingness to respond to her reflects his view of the boundaries of his ministry, made especially pronounced by his statement: "I was sent only to the lost sheep of the House of Israel."

In both versions, the disciples are embarrassed and annoyed by the woman. They urge Jesus to act—either to send her away or to give her what she wants to stop the commotion.[101] Jesus's resistance to the woman intensifies her persistence and courage. Mathew shows how unwilling she

---

[99] Op. cit., *NRSV*, Matthew 15:21-28

[100] Op. cit., *MSG*, p. 179

[101] The Greek can be interpreted both ways.

is to be intimidated. She shifts her tone, kneels before him, and pleads. But Jesus does not give in.

The Story Continues

The next comment of Jesus appears in both versions, and it contains the harshest language in the New Testament:

It is not fair to take the children's food and throw it to the dogs.

Our image of a compassionate Jesus is tested by this remark: his behavior is unloving and cold. Yet for many, this story validates the true humanity of Jesus. Helen Burch Pearson provides this helpful explanation of Jesus's comments: to Jews, "dogs were dirty, unpleasant wild animals" who "roamed the streets in packs scrounging for food." They would never be allowed near the table.[102]

In Matthew, despite being rebuffed a third time, the woman presses him further and employs Jesus's own words to emphasize her point. And she succeeds. She is prepared to beg like a dog. And though she is a Gentile whose culture holds a special fondness for dogs as household pets,[103] she uses her cleverness to reinforce the intensity of her faith so that Jesus relents and heals her absent daughter immediately.

Guided Meditation

Imagine the desperation of this mother whose daughter has been invaded by an unclean spirit.

---

[102]   Op. cit., Pearson, p. 80.
[103]   Op. cit., Pearson, p. 82.

Notice how her hopes rise when she hears that a man has arrived in town who has divine healing powers. Imagine how she garners her courage and strength to ask Jesus to heal her daughter.

Consider Jesus's annoyance when she pesters him. Note how he chooses to ignore her.

Imagine her growing insistence and unwillingness to give up.

Listen closely to their banter. Imagine how Jesus and the woman must have felt about the other.

Notice how the woman finally gets his attention and admiration. Imagine her sense of accomplishment and triumph.

Reflection Questions

When you have wanted something from God, did you get discouraged when your prayers seemed to go unanswered? Or did you persevere?

In the future, if you model your behavior after this persistent mother, would that change the way you make your requests to Jesus or to God?

What advice would you give others who need God's help?

Conclusions

Though she is described by Mark as a Syro-Phoenician woman, Matthew labels her a Canaanite. Both authors emphasize that she is an ethnic and religious outsider. Matthew's Canaanite label is puzzling because Canaanites had ceased to exist in Jesus's time. An explanation may be found, however, in the fact that the Canaanites were remembered as "the indigenous people with whom the Israelites battled for the 'promised land.'" [104] As such, she is portrayed as unclean and impure, an enemy of his people—and Jesus says his compassion is reserved for the lost sheep of Israel.

In Matthew's version, the woman addresses Jesus as "Lord, Son of David," which indicates trust in his divine authority"[105] even though she is an outsider. In fact, she addresses him as *Lord* three times, suggesting perhaps that he is Lord of the Gentiles as well as Lord of the Jews.

The woman believes that Jesus can cure her daughter. Although she may not know a lot about him or the Messianic hopes of the Hebrew people, she knows that her daughter needs his help. It is this trust combined with her persistence that reveals her faith. Jesus honors her confidence in him, and her belief in what Frances Gench calls the "inclusive power, presence and mercy of God."[106]

In Matthew's story, Jesus's final response to the woman is very direct. Speaking to her for the first time, he says, "Woman, great is your faith. Let it be done to you as you wish."

This incident reminds me of the story Jesus tells when his disciples ask him to teach them how to pray. Jesus describes a homeowner who is visited at midnight. He seeks food from his neighbor's cupboard to feed them. His neighbor has already gone to bed and refuses to get up. Despite the neighbor's

---

[104] Op. cit., Gench, p. 6.
[105] Ibid., Gench, p. 6.
[106] Ibid., Gench, p. 110.

refusal, he does not stop knocking or asking for what he and his guests need. Eventually, the neighbor gets out of bed and brings the needed food from his cupboard. After telling this story, Jesus tells his disciples that they must be persistent when they pray to ensure that they will be answered. [107]

Like the other stories of Jesus's healings, this story witnesses to the extraordinary power at work in him. With Simon Peter's mother-in-law, Jesus used physical contact to heal her. With the woman with a hemorrhage, touching his clothing was sufficient. In this story, the girl is healed even though she is not physically present. Here, Jesus accomplishes the healing through his spoken word and intention.

This incident grants Jesus a wider audience who have a greater appreciation of the universality of his message and healing gifts. His powers are no longer the exclusive privilege of the Judean people; his mission is extended to all. Whereas the initial rebuff of the woman by Jesus reflects his belief in the priority of his mission to the Jews, his reconsideration of the Greek mother's insistent request reminds us that God's dominion (and therefore, the church's mission) is to all people, especially those who are not yet inside our doors!

The Syro-Phoenician (or Canaanite) woman is a model for all women who seek a seat at the table instead of remaining on the sidelines. Such women include feminist biblical scholars and those seeking women's ordination or consecration as bishops in Christian communities—as well as women seeking justice today. Elisabeth Schussler-Fiorenza urges Christian feminists to heed the example of Mathew's Canaanite woman, noting that "she does not enter the house and interrupt Jesus (as in Mark); rather she 'comes out' and 'shouts after Jesus's and his disciples.'"[108] She urges women today to position themselves "in the public-political center of the church and the academy."[109]

---

[107] The late Walter Wink made this point in several of his programs that I attended.

[108] Elisabeth Schussler-Fiorenza, *But She Said*, p. 103.

[109] Ibid., Schussler-Fiorenza, p. 103.

Schussler-Fiorenza also warns that, though this woman's argument convinces Jesus to heal her daughter, she accomplishes her goal without arguing for equality. In other words, she begs for crumbs like a second-class citizen! She concludes that, on the one hand, this is a sacred text that advocates women's assertiveness, but on the other hand it "reinscribes patriarchal power-relations" and "feminine submissive behavior."

This is the only instance in the Gospels when Jesus changes his mind, and it is not insignificant that his mind is altered by a woman who should not be speaking to him at all. Like her, we all want to be assured that our faith is strong enough to survive the crises we are presented with and that God is with us, whoever we are. Empowered by faith, her hopes are fulfilled. She is an intercessor who calls us all to reach out on behalf of those in need.

Remember now those individuals who have interceded for others and for *you* during your life. Thank God for them.

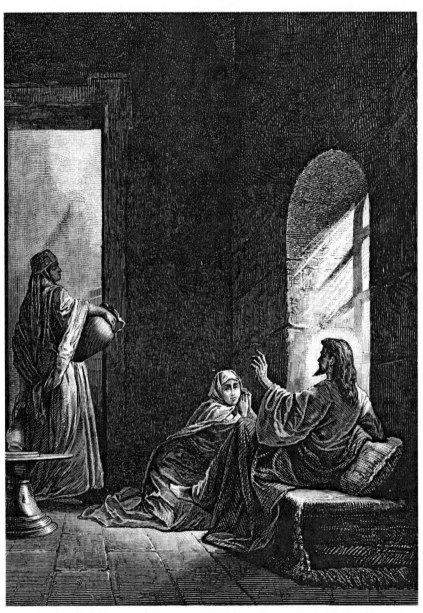

Image 12: Mary and Martha Welcome Jesus into Their Home

CHAPTER 12:
MARY AND MARTHA WELCOME JESUS

There are many stories in the Gospels that describe dinners that Jesus shared with others. One of the most famous is Luke's description of the time when Mary and Martha of Bethany welcomed Jesus into their home. Here is Luke's description[110]:

> Now, as they went on their way, Jesus entered a certain village, where a woman named Martha welcomed him into her home. She had a sister named Mary, who sat at the Lord's feet and listened to what he was saying. But Martha was distracted by her many tasks; so she came to [Jesus] and asked, "Lord, do you not care that my sister has left me to do all the work by myself? Tell her then to help me." But the Lord answered her, "Martha, Martha, you are worried and distracted by many things; there is need of only one thing. Mary has chosen the better part, which will not be taken away from her."

Comments

Most first-century women believed that their place was in the home and that their primary task was service. Women spent most of their time preparing meals, making clothes, doing laundry, and tending to the children. However, those roles were restrictive and often demeaned. They heard the men say these sorts of daily thanksgiving prayers:

> Praised be God that you did not make me a Gentile; praised be God that you did not make me a woman;

---

[110]   Op. cit., *NRSV*, Luke 10:38–42, p. 72.

praised be God that you did not create me an ignorant man.[111]

Women saw men study and discuss the Scripture with a rabbi and "sit at his feet" as he explained it. Eliezer, a first-century rabbi, advised the men as follows: "Rather should the words of the Torah be burned than entrusted to a woman."[112]

Because women were not allowed to study the Scripture, Mary's actions and the approval Jesus gives to her inclusion as he taught is extraordinary. He is unequivocal in his statement that women have a right to study theology and the Scripture like the men; they do not have to be confined to domestic tasks.

Mary exhibits an openness to the Word and work of God and the mission of Jesus; she is an example of a listening disciple. Listening and hearing the Word is valued by Jesus and is reported in other contexts in the Gospel of Luke.[113] Mary's focused concentration on Jesus contrasts sharply with Martha's harried distraction. Although Mary's behavior provokes the dialogue, she doesn't speak; only the dialogue between Jesus and Martha is recorded. Martha interrupts Jesus while he is teaching and demands that Jesus intervene. She says emphatically, *"My* sister has left *me* to do all the work by *myself.* Tell her to help *me."* In a delightful retelling of this story, David Redding hears the following message in Jesus's reply: "No Martha, I'm not going to help you control Mary. God's going to be Mary's boss from now on, not you."[114]

The climax is found in the reply Jesus gives to Martha's request. Jesus is telling Martha much more than the fact that she does not have to prepare a feast to please him; he also is telling her that listening to his counsel and

---

[111] A quotation from Tosephta, Ber. 7, 18 and Talmud, pBer. 13b; bMen. 43b cited by Swidler, p. 18.

[112] A quotation from Mishnah, Sota 3, 4 cited by Swidler, p. 18.

[113] See Luke 2:19, 2:51, 6:46–49, 8:15, 8:21, 11:28.

[114] Op. cit., Redding, p. 41.

understanding his teachings are more important than her hostess chores. He chides her about her anxiety regarding so many tasks and distractions:

> "Martha, Martha, you are worried and distracted by many things; there is need of only one thing. Mary has chosen the better part, which will not be taken away from her."[115]

In telling Martha that "there is need of only one thing,"[116] Jesus shows his preference for attentive disciples and sharply contrasts her choice with that of her sister. Elsewhere, Luke indicates that Jesus believes that anxiety is an impediment to discipleship. In Luke 12:22–31, Jesus specifically tells his disciples "not to worry or be anxious." A complete trust in God can banish anxiety.

Luke's Gospel contains many female characters and many passages that deal with women. In fact, nearly one-third of the material that is unique to Luke concerns women. Several of the stories in Luke where women are prominent also appear in Mark, but they have been redacted to serve Luke's purposes.[117]

This story is found only in the Gospel of Luke, where it is positioned after Jesus tells the lawyer that, in order to inherit eternal life, he must commit to the two great commandments: to love God with all your heart, soul, strength, and mind, and to love your neighbor as yourself. Luke then tells two stories: the story of the Good Samaritan, which exemplifies neighborly love, and the story that includes the visit to Mary and Martha's home (where Mary sits at Jesus's feet in the posture of a loving, attentive disciple). Martha's welcome also expresses her embrace of Jesus's mission and her desire to contribute to it. However, her preoccupation with kitchen preparations diverts her from the lessons he is teaching.

---

[115] Op. cit., *NRSV*, Luke 10:41b–42, p. 72.

[116] Op. cit., *NRSV*, Luke 10:42, p. 72.

[117] Op. cit., Thurston, pp. 100–102.

Because the goal of Jesus is to develop disciples, he approves of Mary as a willing candidate, even though it is a unique role for a woman in his time. Jesus is telling Martha to shift her priorities, to let go of the culturally based feminine edicts and further her preparation as *one* of his female disciples. Jesus is saying, "You have to listen to me, hear the Word, and digest it if you want to follow me."

Two thousand years later, whenever and wherever the role choices for women are debated, the story of Mary and Martha is often used to support one side over the other. Such interpretations are reductive and lose the context and intent of the story. Still, these sorts of analyses are expected in a world where female roles are so strongly contested. When audiences today hear Jesus's preference for Mary's choice, some feel honored. Some even regard this story as one of the most liberating texts in the Gospels.[118] Others find it offensive because they believe Jesus's words devalue the hospitality offered to him by Martha, hospitality that Jesus and his disciples depended upon numerous times.[119]

Guided Meditation

Meals can mark special times: celebrations, holidays, meetings with friends and family, or quiet times with loved ones. Close your eyes for a few minutes and remember a meal that you prepared or hosted that was really special for you. Reflect on why it was special.

Imagine yourself sitting at Jesus's feet and listening like Mary. Now reflect on what that is like.

---

[118] Op. cit., Gench, p. 56
[119] Ibid., Gench, p. 57

Imagine yourself as Martha. What do you notice?

Reflection Questions

Do you experience some of the same competing interests as Martha?

Does this quarrel among the two sisters remind you of your own family? How?

Does one of these two women best represent you?

Are you comfortable with your resemblance to that woman?

Or do you see yourself resembling both of them? Why?

What do you do to welcome Jesus into your home and your life?

Do you give yourself time to learn from Jesus?

How can we learn to be more present to Christ and to the Christ in each other?

The Importance of This Story to the Early Church

In the years after Jesus's death, the story of Mary and Martha was a reminder to women who hosted Eucharistic gatherings in their homes to focus on Christ's presence and not to worry about material concerns.

In the Pauline churches, women held important roles as heads of house churches and preachers. However, Luke's church returned to more socially accepted roles for women.[120] When the Gospel of Luke was written, significant events had occurred that affected the developing Christian community. Scholar Mary Ann Getty-Sullivan asserts that Luke is trying "to show that Christian life is compatible with the social patterns of Rome-administered Judea and Galilee."[121] In support of Getty-Sullivan, Frances Gench adds that *diakonia* in Luke consistently refers to domestic service, such as providing food, not ecclesial leadership.[122] Gench says that, though women are more evident in Luke's Gospel, "they are presented in carefully circumscribed roles, primarily as nurturers and benefactors, who support the ministry of Jesus and his disciples." They "are never referred to as 'disciples' or 'apostles,'" nor do they proclaim the Word publicly, as the men do.[123]

---

[120]   Op. cit., Getty-Sullivan, p. 194.

[121]   Ibid., Getty-Sullivan, p. 194.

[122]   Op. cit., Gench, p. 66.

[123]   Ibid., Gench, p. 68. In fact, in Luke's version of the empty tomb, Jesus does not appear first to women and women are not commissioned (as in Matthew and John).

One feminist scholar, Elizabeth Schussler Fiorenza, takes a different posture. She notes that this story reflects "the struggle of early Christian women against patriarchal restrictions of their leadership and ministry at the turn of the first century."[124] She views Martha as the leader of a house church who welcomed Jesus as an equal into her home and offered *diakonia* (service), which is a part of any Christian ministry.[125] Other critics justifiably challenge Schussler Fiorenza's construct of Mary as a passive listener because her refusal to engage in the traditional role of service in order to learn from Jesus is bold for her time.

It may be the author of Luke, not Jesus, who wants to silence female leaders of house churches by praising Mary's subordinate behavior in his own community. But all of these explanations go beyond the text, and although they result from careful examination of the texts and their translations,[126] I believe they miss Jesus's priorities regarding women's roles as disciples.

Conclusions

Luke's account suggests that Jesus is welcomed into the home of two autonomous women, which is most unusual given the times. In John's Gospel, the sisters have a brother named Lazarus, who is not mentioned by Luke. Lazarus is the man that Jesus later raises from the dead after fervent pleas by the two sisters.

Because the Revised Common Lectionary assigns this story to be the Gospel for the eleventh Sunday after Pentecost in Year C, preachers often give Mary an aura of holiness. Conversely, Martha is personified as the housekeeper. Thus, churches often refer to some women as the "Martha type," meaning they are practical, competent, and organized. Those called the "Mary type" are usually quiet, restrained, and good at listening. As previously stated, I don't think this was Jesus's intent. In Martha's home,

---

[124] Op. cit., Schussler Fiorenza, p. 68.
[125] Op. cit., Gench, p. 66.
[126] Op. cit., Gench describes these textual difficulties on pp. 62–63.

Jesus was a special guest. In this particular instance, Martha is too busy with hosting to benefit from his teaching.

Taking time to listen and reflect is important for all of us, even as we are required to complete those tasks that keep our lives working effectively and our ministries successful. Martha's situation is a good reminder to those of us immersed in ministry that the words of Jesus are the essential resource we are given to inspire our work. It tells us that when Jesus comes, we should stop what we are doing and be attentive! Perhaps we should all follow the ideal of Bernard of Clairvaux of a "mixed life" of active charity and contemplative prayer, which is also the hallmark of the Franciscans. Stated simply, take time in your life to listen to Jesus and put what you have learned into practice. If our service is so great that we become anxious, preoccupied, and inattentive, we become out of balance and need replenishment, which silence and reflection on the Word provide. The life of a disciple requires both hearing and doing; Jesus claims members of his family are "those who hear the word of God and do it."[127]

---

[127] Op. cit., *NRSV*, Luke 8:21, p. 67.

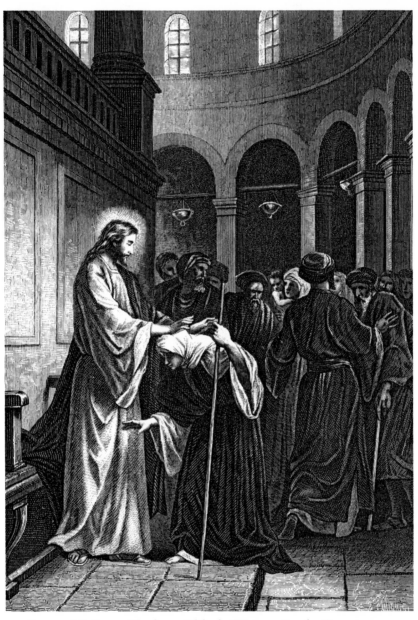

Image 13: Jesus Heals an Elderly Woman in the Synagogue

CHAPTER 13:
JESUS HEALS A BENT-OVER WOMAN

One Sabbath, while Jesus is teaching in one of the synagogues, he notices a woman who is so crippled that she is bent over and can not look up. This is what Luke says about what Jesus said and did:

> Now [Jesus] was teaching in one of the synagogues on the sabbath. And just then there appeared a woman with a spirit that had crippled her for eighteen years. She was bent over and was quite unable to stand up straight. When Jesus saw her, he called her over and said, "Woman, you are set free from your ailment." When he laid his hands on her, immediately she stood up straight and began praising God. But the leader of the synagogue, indignant because Jesus had cured on the sabbath, kept saying to the crowd, "There are six days on which work ought to be done, come on those days and be cured, and not on the sabbath day." But [Jesus] answered him and said, "You hypocrites! Does not each of you on the sabbath untie his ox or his donkey from the manger and lead it away to give it water? And ought not this woman, a daughter of Abraham whom Satan bound for eighteen long years, be set free from this bondage on the sabbath day?" When he said this, all his opponents were put to shame, and the entire crowd was rejoicing at all the wonderful things that he was doing.[128]

---

[128] Op. cit., *NRSV*, Luke 13:10–17, p. 76.

Guided Meditation

In order to imagine the experience of this woman, you need to replicate the state of her deformed body. Stand up now and bend your body at the waist so that all you see is what is below you.

You may see the floor, your own feet and some furniture. Notice that your view of the world is limited.

Recognize the limits of the crippled woman's vision and identify what you were able to see from that bent-over position.

You may become light-headed if you remain in that bent-over position for too long. Stand up straight and then sit down. Identify the ways your body felt when it was twisted and constrained in that position

If *you* have to live your life bent over, like this elderly woman, *you* will not be able to greet people or see their faces or share their joys and sorrows.

You placed your body in that awkward and uncomfortable position for only a few moments – imagine being this way for eighteen years!

When *you* are in that position, you can not see Jesus, even if he is directly in front of you. But he can see you.

Imagine being that woman, encountering Jesus and see him take the initiative by greeting *you* and healing *you*.

When he says, "Woman, you are set free from your ailment," *your* misery comes to an end. Can *you* feel the joy and gratitude the once-crippled woman feels when Jesus sets her body free?

All of life is suddenly opened up before her. Imagine her response.

Stand up again and bend over like the woman. Imagine Jesus laying his hands on you.

With his hands, he is extending God's healing power to you.

By acting on the Sabbath, he is risking his own well-being.

When Jesus enables you to stand upright, you can look into his eyes. Imagine that.

If you have a picture of Jesus, stand before it. His eyes are warm, gentle and kind; his face is full of compassion. If you are the woman he has healed, what do you want to say?

Reflection Questions

Think about your own life now. Have you experienced that kind of immediate transformation and freedom?

Write about it here.

Have you witnessed that kind of transformation in another? Write about it here.

Are you yearning to be free of your infirmities? Explain.

In what ways are you like the healing Jesus?

Comments

This story places the woman in the synagogue on the Sabbath. Luke's mention of her presence suggests that she, like other women of her time, regularly took part in the synagogue worship and teaching. The description of her crippled body makes her presence there even more poignant. Helen Burch Pearson notes that, in the first century, possession by a spirit of infirmity meant that the person "was to be avoided at all costs; for to aid her in any way was to assist the work of Satan" and "risk invasion by the evil spirits." She adds, "Those who were overcome by unclean spirits were believed to be guilty of disobedience to God's will."[129]

When Jesus calls out to her, he makes her visible to everybody. By doing that, he defies the prohibition that kept men from speaking to women in public. Also, he is unafraid to touch a woman he does not know, even though she might be unclean or transmit her demons.

Jesus refers to her as a daughter of Abraham, one of God's chosen people, who is worth far more than any animal they might care for. Whereas *son of Abraham* is a common phrase used throughout Hebrew and Jewish literature, the term *daughter of Abraham* is rarely if ever applied

---

[129] Op. cit., Pearson, p. 58

to women.[130] For Jesus, women are full participants of the people and covenant of God.

The bent-over woman was perceived by many to have had little value and to be of little use for eighteen years. Her healing empowered her suddenly to achieve her full potential. Pearson reminds us that the mission of Jesus "was to save, and this meant to heal and make whole."[131] The elderly woman's condition called for immediate action; Jesus would not consider waiting until after the Sabbath.

The healing of this crippled woman also affirms that the value of a woman is as great as that of a man. When this woman is healed, Peterson's *The Message* describes her reaction this way:

"Suddenly, she was standing straight and tall, giving glory to God."[132]

Reflection Questions

Think about yourself. Are there psychological wounds in need of healing that keep you from realizing your hopes and dreams?

[130] Op. cit., Swidler, p. 63
[131] Ibid., Pearson, p. 58
[132] Op. cit., *MSG*, LUKE 13: 13, p. 1897

Did over-critical parents or parent figures make you feel unworthy or squash your self-esteem?

Did sexual abuse or trauma leave you feeling unable to master life's challenges?

In what ways are you like the bent-over woman?

Comments

There are professionals in the psychological community today who can undo the harmful effects of childhood mistreatment and trauma. If you need that help but haven't searched out those resources, I urge you to do so now.

In their books and trainings, psychologists Kristen Neff and Christopher Germer describe a different way of relating to ourselves that involves self-compassion, which has a profound healing effect.[133] Learning to treat ourselves with "loving kindness" is the love of self that Jesus taught.

Conclusions

The controversy that arose after the healing was caused by how the Sabbath Law was interpreted. The synagogue leader insisted that the healing was work, which is strictly forbidden on the Sabbath. Instead of directly criticizing Jesus, the synagogue leader scolded the crippled woman for stopping by on the Sabbath. He was more concerned with the letter of the law than its spirit. The endless study of the Sabbath Law led the Jewish religious leaders to add to the rules they believed a devout Jew had to keep. Jesus understood that additional laws didn't draw people closer to God; rather, they made the relationship more difficult. Jesus sees his actions as compassionate, which falls outside the prohibitions of the Sabbath Law.

Calling him a hypocrite, Jesus rebukes the synagogue leader and defends his actions and the woman's healing. He says that, even on the Sabbath, God's work must be done. Jesus is presenting himself as a new authority on the Sabbath Law, and he shifts it from a rigid set of Sabbath rules to more humane regulations. The healing act of Jesus and his teaching set them all free from enslavement to a tradition that placed more importance on following the rules than on responding to the welfare and needs of human beings. He challenged the use of Mosaic Law and its

---

[133]   Neff, Kristin, *Self-Compassion* and Germer, Christopher, *Mindful Self-Compassion*.

traditions that kept some bent over and burdened. Jesus knew that no one was free as long as some remained crippled.

This healing affected the whole assembly that day. "The entire crowd was rejoicing at all the wonderful things that he (Jesus) was doing."[134, 135]

Jesus demonstrates that compassion is not just a feeling. In fact, it is an action based on feelings. He calls on us to be more compassionate toward those in need, wherever we find ourselves. To make justice for all a reality in the twenty-first century will require all our effort. Every person who remains bent over keeps the rest of us from standing upright.[136]

---

[134] Op. cit., *NRSV*, Luke 13:17, p. 76.
[135] Op. cit., Pearson, p. 57.
[136] Ibid., Pearson, p. 55.

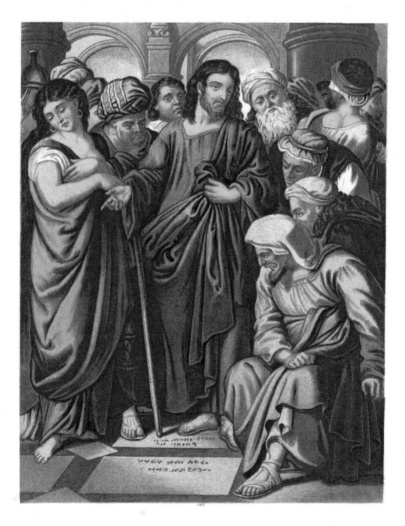

THE WOMAN TAKEN IN ADULTERY.

**Image 14: Rendering of Jesus Defending
'The Woman Taken in Adultery'**

CHAPTER 14:
A WOMAN ACCUSED OF ADULTERY
IS BROUGHT TO JESUS

The Gospel of John includes a story of a woman who has been accused of adultery. It is a story that has aroused a lot of controversy over the centuries because there is little agreement on its meaning. The story begins early in the morning, when Jesus returns to the Temple and is greeted by a crowd of people. After sitting down to teach them, he is interrupted:

> The Scribes and Pharisees brought a woman who had been caught in adultery and making her stand before all of them, they said to him, "Teacher, this woman was caught in the very act of committing adultery. Now in the law, Moses commanded us to stone such women. Now, what do you say?" They said this to test him, so that they might have some charge to bring against him. Jesus bent down and wrote with his finger on the ground. When they kept on questioning him, he straightened up and said to them, "Let anyone among you who is without sin be the first to throw a stone at her." And once again he bent down and wrote on the ground. When they heard it, they went away, one by one, beginning with the elders; and Jesus was left alone with the woman standing before him. Jesus straightened up and said to her, "Woman, where are they? Has no one condemned you?" She said, "No one, sir." And Jesus said, "Neither do I condemn you. Go your way, and from now on do not sin again."[137]

---

[137] Op. cit., *NRSV*, John 8: 2–11, pp. 100–101.

<u>Comments</u>

Here, a private situation is made public. As such, it becomes subject to public condemnation. The law regarding adultery is spelled out in Leviticus 20:10 and Deuteronomy 22:22–24, which states that *both* the woman and the man who have committed adultery are to be put to death by stoning. The accusers in this story make no reference to the man involved in the act. The proposed punishment is directed solely toward the woman. Some scholars believe that the absence of the male participant is a sign of the double standard associated with sexuality. It is also possible that the woman has been entrapped.

To be in a seated position at the beginning conveys that Jesus is a teacher of the Law. The woman, for whom this is a life-and-death situation, is seen by many to be a pawn for the Scribes and Pharisees in their challenge of Jesus. These religious authorities want to see whether Jesus will uphold the law or deviate from it. One of the charges against Jesus "is that he forgave sin on his own authority."[138] They know Jesus professes a law based on love as well as obedience to God. Here is their challenge: if Jesus favors stoning her, they can question his compassion and assert that he will be in violation of Roman law, which limited the authority to impose capital punishment to the Roman government. If he says she should not be stoned, they can accuse him of disobeying the Mosaic Law. In other words, his answer may give them something they can use against him.

Whenever Jesus sat in the Temple and taught, he was encroaching on the authority and power of the official rabbis, Pharisees, and scribes who represented the most dedicated and knowledgeable men in Jewish circles at that time. They are faithful to all the Laws of Moses and regularly worship in the Temple. Their self-righteousness is evident in their accusation.

In this situation, with just a few words, Jesus transforms their rigid Mosaic thinking with its absolutes into a view that is based on interpretation, individual responsibility, and equal justice. This is Jesus's message whether you are the woman accused of adultery or those standing in front of a pile of stones.

---

[138] Op. cit., Getty-Sullivan, p. 101.

Guided Meditation

Picture the woman, standing alone in front of her accusers. She says nothing, but that doesn't mean that she is without thoughts or feelings. Imagine her feelings.

After hearing their accusations, Jesus responds by turning away and bending down to write with his finger on the ground. What do you suppose he is doing?

Jesus's actions suggest that, for whatever reason, he is either choosing to disengage from the accusers, refraining from standing with them, or taking time for reflection before he speaks. Imagine his thought processes.

When the woman's accusers continue to ask questions of Jesus, he stands up and challenges them in terms of their own ethical conduct: "Let anyone among you who is without sin, be the first to throw a stone at her." Imagine this.

Jesus is taking a stand that no one expected. Imagine his insight and courage.

Watch the accusers as they take in Jesus's challenge. Imagine how each individual responds to this.

Comments

In a recent book, Stephen Binz points out that, normally, the witnesses are the first to throw a stone. In other words, the accusers typically serve as executioners. Here, "the accusers become the accused."[139] If they chose to throw a stone and deny their own sin, they would be committing blasphemy. If they did not, they would be admitting that they were guilty of sin. Jesus made it their choice, not his.[140] Many scholars think that Jesus is applying Exodus 23:1, 7 "to remind his hearers of what the law required; 'a wicked man, one who hated his brother in his heart or one whose motives were devious, could neither accuse, nor testify, nor condemn.'"[141]

Without waiting for the first stone to be thrown, Jesus again turns away, bends over, and uses his finger to write on the ground. No one accepts Jesus's invitation to cast the first stone. To everyone's amazement, each of them goes away, one by one, beginning with the elders. The scribes and Pharisees have judged themselves guilty![142]

---

[139] Binz, Stephen J. *Women of the Gospels,* p. 118.

[140] Op. cit., Pearson p. 129.

[141] Op. cit. Barrett, p. 590.

[142] Ibid., Pearson, p. 121.

Guided Meditation

Jesus is now alone with the woman. Look closely at the woman standing before him. Even though she has been exposed, she has said nothing to justify her actions, nor is she contrite. When her accusers walk away, she remains quiet. What might she be thinking?

There are many characters in this story: Jesus, the accused woman, the elders, the Pharisees, and the Scribes. Do you identify with any of them? Who and why?

When everyone has walked away, Jesus returns to a standing position, looks at the woman, and asks her directly, "Woman, where are they? Has no one condemned you?" She speaks for the first time, "No one, sir." And then Jesus adds, "Neither do I condemn you," and he tells her to go. He also adds, "From now on, do not sin again."[143] Imagine the woman's response to Jesus's words.

God did not send Jesus into the world to condemn; he came to save the world.[144] That offer of new beginnings and new life is given to us. Can you accept his offer?

---

[143] Op. cit., *NRSV*, John 8: 10b–11, p. 101.
[144] Op. cit., *NRSV*, John 3:17.

What is Jesus telling you to stop doing?

Does his promise make you want to confess your sins and begin a new life? Explain.

Jesus understands that none of us is free from criticism or judgment. We receive it from others and apply it toward others. But he wants us to be more sensitive to our own sinfulness so that we can be more compassionate and accepting of others and ourselves. Our judgments provide the fuel for racism, sexism, hatred of gays and transgendered people, ageism, and neglect of the poor. When you find yourself about to judge and criticize someone or some group, how can you remember Jesus's saying—"Let anyone among you who is without sin, be the first to throw a stone"—and stop yourself?

Reflection Questions

Even today, women are subject to more criticism about the display of their bodies, their attire, and their sexuality than men in our society. In spite of action to improve their treatment by police, lawyers, and the other officials, a female victim of rape is often subjected to humiliation and suspicion regarding whether her behavior was seductive or provocative. Have you ever been humiliated or condemned for your sexuality?

Today, young girls who wear tight sweaters, makeup, short skirts, or skinny pants receive all kinds of negative labels. In most cases, they are only replicating what they see in the media, but others feel free to gossip about them. Young women continue to be raised to be careful about their reputations and distrustful of male intentions. What will it take to level the playing field?

Guided Meditation for Women

If you are a woman, please take some time now to look at how you see yourself. Get comfortable and quiet down. As you inhale and exhale slowly, follow your breathing. Pay attention to your body. If you feel tension anywhere, notice it and let it go.

Truly, your body is a gift from God, and God loves you the way you are. Some people, including you, may not believe that. Remember a time when you were shamed because of your body or when you were afraid because of your body. Where were you? Let your mind remember the scene. Who made you feel ashamed of your body?

Now imagine that Jesus has come into the scene that you are remembering. He appears quiet and calm. When the shaming words are said to you, he speaks. What do you hear him say?

After Jesus speaks, your accuser leaves. Only you and Jesus remain. His eyes are warm and kind. He says, "Do not be afraid. We all make mistakes. Sometimes our behavior is misinterpreted. Whatever the case, know that God loves you. Go on your way knowing that you have been made whole." Rest awhile with that imagined scene and then take time to journal about it.

Did that experience make a difference in how you see yourself?

Do you know that God loves you?

In the past, did you think God's love was contingent upon your behavior?

Did you ever promise to be good in exchange for God's forgiveness?

Now shift your attention to Jesus. What does this scene tell you about Jesus?

How Different Commentators See This Text

There is as much disagreement among the interpreters of this text as there is agreement. So many important points have been made that I have chosen to present all their opinions for your consideration.

Most biblical scholars believe that the story of the woman accused of adultery was not a part of the Gospel of John originally because it does not appear in the earliest Greek manuscripts of John's Gospel. It came into the canonical scriptures through the Western Latin Church, although there is reference to the story in the third-century *Didascalia* of Syrian origin.[145] In later Greek manuscripts, the story appears in various locations in John and Luke. Frances Gench points out that, in terms of vocabulary, style, and theology, it is more like Luke's writings than John's.[146] Whatever its source, scholars believe that this story is an ancient one from the oral tradition.[147]

Gench and other scholars suggest that its delayed placement may have to do with the ease with which Jesus extended mercy to this adulterous woman, which was difficult for the early church to reconcile with their severe stance against sexual offenses. The story could have been an embarrassment to them because they may have thought it suggested

---

[145] Op cit, Swidler, p. 66.
[146] Op. cit., Gench, p. 136.
[147] Ibid., Gench, p. 137.

to women that they could live sinful lives. But Bonnie Thurston asks alternatively, "Was their concern what would happen if female sexuality passed out of male control?"[148]

When none of the Jewish authorities elect to cast the first stone, it is a sign that Jesus's instruction to them has changed them. Brad H. Young, a scholar of first-century Judaism, cited by Gench,[149] omits John 8:6a—"They said this to test him, so that they might have some charge against him"—from the text, which presents a different read on this story. [150] He notes, "Many of the traditional readings of the story of the adulteress seem in conflict with what is known about Pharisaic attitudes and practices" because they were reluctant to use capital punishment. He adds, "When a difficult religious issue arises in the life of the community which affects faith and practice, it was an accepted practice to seek a *responsum*."[151] A *responsum* provided a forum in which questions and answers were raised concerning biblical interpretation. Young concludes that the problem posed to Jesus was such a question. For Young, the whole episode portrays the oral tradition as a living Torah, which is adapted and applied in everyday life situations.[152]

A feminist Japanese scholar, Hisako Kinukawa, notes that, by identifying the scribes and Pharisees as sinners along with the woman, Jesus saves her from the punishment of death; however, Jesus fails to raise important questions such as why the woman was exposed but not the man and what factors led to the adulterous act.[153] During that time, adultery was a violation of property rights. It was unlawful because it entailed the

---

[148] Op. cit., Thurston, p. 87.

[149] Op. cit., Gench, p. 145.

[150] Brad H. Young, "'Save the Adulteress!' Ancient Jewish *Responsa* in the Gospels? *New Testament Studies* 41, (1995), pp. 59–70.

[151] Ibid., Young, p. 65.

[152] Ibid., Young, p. 67.

[153] Hisako Kinukawa, "On John 7:53–8:11: A Well-Cherished But Much Clouded Story" in *Readings from this Place, Vol. 2, Social Location and Biblical Interpretation in Global Perspective*, Fernando F. Segovia and Mary Ann Tolbert (Eds.), pp. 82–96.

theft of another man's property—that is, a wife was the possession of her husband. By committing adultery, she not only disobeyed him, she also introduced the possibility that her husband may not receive a proper heir.[154] A man's adultery was only a crime if he seduced a married or betrothed woman.[155]

Alan Watson adds to our quandary about this text. He raises the possibility that the woman may have been a remarried divorcee because Jesus declared that a woman whose husband divorced her and then remarried committed adultery.[156] Moses, on the other hand, allowed divorce. The scribes and Pharisees may have brought this woman to Jesus for this reason. Gench adds that Watson's arguments may explain the many unexplained features of the story—that is, why the woman was not formally tried, why Jesus accepts that she is guilty, why no evidence or witnesses are presented (including her partner in crime), and why the scribes and Pharisees brought her to Jesus.[157] If the woman is a remarried divorcée, there would be no adultery and no male adulterer under Pharisaic ethics.

Holly J. Toensing raises additional questions that merit our consideration. She argues that Jesus does not treat the Jewish leaders and the woman as equals. He does not challenge that sin in patriarchal societies is defined differently for males and females. Whereas married men could have sex with any woman who was not engaged or married, a married woman could only have sex with her husband. He allows the men to engage in self-evaluation, but he addresses the woman with a command on how to behave according to male standards.[158] Furthermore, he never uses the language of forgiveness in addressing the woman, nor does the woman express repentance or faith. Jesus shows her mercy and calls her

---

[154] Lucy Fuchs, *We Were There, Women in the New Testament,* p. 58.

[155] Op. cit., Pearson, p. 127. (In Exodus 20:17, a wife is listed along with the rest of a man's property.)

[156] Alan Watson, "Jesus and the Adulteress" *Biblica* 80 (1999), p. 102.

[157] Op. cit., Gench, p. 151

[158] 162 Toensing, Holly J. "Divine Interventions or Divine Intrusions." (Cited by Gench, Op. cit., pp. 151–152.)
163 Ibid., Toensing, cited by Gench, pp. 151–152.

to righteousness. Simply put, he lets her go free.[159] His actions will never satisfy those who would condemn her, nor will they satisfy those who yearn for Jesus to challenge the double standards of the sexual behavior of men and women.[160]

Conclusions

Noteworthy, is the fact that Jesus treats the woman as a person rather than as a temptress or sexual predator. He recognizes that the woman has sinned, but he refuses to let the guilt of sin define her. He tells her to stop engaging in an adulterous relationship and gives her the possibility of a new relationship with God. She is free and told to live free from sin. And so are her accusers: Jesus offers them the same new life he offers her.

The law in Deuteronomy 17:7 deals only with the guilt of the one accused, not with the guilt of the accuser. Jesus presents a different principle: if you wish to accuse others, you must be without reproach yourself. This is how he highlights the importance of seeing ourselves as sinners, which can heal our judgmental hearts and enable us to regard others and ourselves with compassion and love. This story continues to witness to the One who redeems the life of both the woman and her accuser.

The woman in this story has no name; instead, she is called only an *adulteress*. She represents all women whose bodies have been demonized as agents of sin. She is the object her accusers have pointed to, and she is described in terms of her sin and the Law. Yet others play a significant role in this story. Jesus also addresses the religious individuals who judge and condemn the one guilty of sexual sin.

Currently, this story of Jesus's response to the woman taken in adultery is *not* included in the Revised Common Lectionary, which governs the selection of biblical readings for mainline churches. I think it would make

---

[159] Leon Morris, *The Gospel According to John, The New International Commentary on the New Testament, rev. ed.,* p. 781.

[160]

a marvelous addition because it encourages us to look at ourselves when we pass judgment. Its absence may be a sign of the masculine bias exercised in choosing the lections for Sundays as well as the diversity of opinion regarding this text.

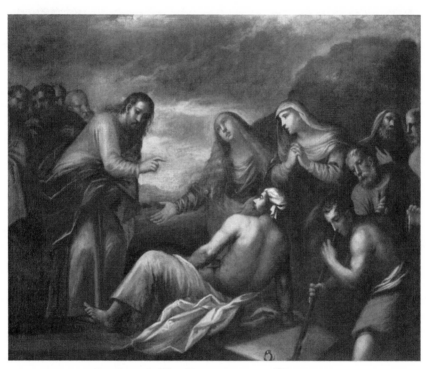

Image 15: The Resurrection of Lazarus

CHAPTER 15:
MARY AND MARTHA BEG JESUS
TO RAISE THEIR BROTHER, LAZARUS

Two central issues arise during the conversation between Jesus and the two sisters of Lazarus, Mary and Martha of Bethany. These conversations highlight that the actions of Jesus in raising Lazarus is a demonstration of God's power to restore life as well as an emotional response to the sisters' loss. This is another story that *only* appears in the Gospel of John. Read it carefully, as if for the first time.

> Now, a certain man was ill, Lazarus of Bethany, the village of Mary and her sister Martha.[161]

> So the sisters sent a message to Jesus, "Lord, he whom you love is ill." But when Jesus heard it, he said, "This illness does not lead to death, rather it is for God's glory, so that the Son of God may be glorified through it." Accordingly, though Jesus loved Martha and her sister and Lazarus, after having heard that Lazarus was ill, he stayed two days longer in the place where he was.

Then after this [Jesus] said to the disciples, "Let us go to Judea again." The disciples said to him, "Rabbi, the Jews were just now trying to stone you, and are you going there again?" Jesus answered, "Are there not twelve hours of daylight? Those who walk during the day do not stumble, because they see the light of this world. But those who walk at night stumble, because the light is not in them." After saying this, he told them, "Our friend Lazarus has fallen asleep, but I am going there to awaken him." The disciples said to him, "Lord, if he has fallen asleep, he will be all right."

---

[161] Op. cit., *NRSV*, John 11:1, p. 104.

Jesus, however, had been speaking about his death, but they thought that he was referring merely to sleep. Then Jesus told them plainly, "Lazarus is dead. For your sake I am glad I was not there, so that you may believe. But let us go to him." Thomas, who was called the Twin, said to his fellow disciples, "Let us also go, that we may die with him."

When Jesus arrived, he found that Lazarus had already been in the tomb four days. Now Bethany was near Jerusalem, some two miles away, and many of the Jews had come to Martha and Mary to console them about their brother. When Martha heard that Jesus was coming, she went and met him, while Mary stayed at home. Martha said to Jesus, "Lord, if you had been here, my brother would not have died. But even now I know that God will give you whatever you ask." Jesus said to her, "Your brother will rise again." Martha said to him, "I know that he will rise again in the resurrection on the last day." Jesus said to her. "I am the resurrection and the life. Those who believe in me, even though they die, will live, and everyone who lives and believes in me will never die. Do you believe this?" She said to him, "Yes, Lord, I believe that you are the Messiah, the Son of God, the one coming into the world."

When she had said this, she went back and called her sister Mary and told her privately, "The Teacher is here and is calling for you." And when she heard it, she got up quickly and went to him. Now Jesus had not yet come to the village, but was still at the place where Martha had met him. The Jews who were with her in the house, consoling her, saw Mary get up quickly and go out. They followed her because they thought she was going to the tomb to weep there. When Mary came where Jesus was and saw him, she knelt at his feet and said to him, "Lord, if you had been here, my brother would not have died." When Jesus saw her weeping, and the Jews who came with her also weeping, he was greatly disturbed in spirit and deeply moved. He said, "Where have you laid him?" They said to him, "Lord, come and see." Jesus began to weep. So the Jews said, "See how he loved him!" But some of them said, "Could not he who opened the eyes of the blind man have kept this man from dying?"

Then Jesus, again gravely disturbed, came to the tomb. It was a cave, and a stone was lying against it. Jesus said, "Take away the stone." Martha, the sister of the dead man, said to him, "Lord, already there is a stench because he has been dead four days." Jesus said to her, "Did I not tell you that if you believed, you would see the glory of God?" So they took away the stone. And Jesus looked upward and said, "[God], I thank you for having heard me. I knew that you always hear me, but I have said this for the sake of the crowd standing here, so that they may believe that you sent me." When he said this, he cried with a loud voice, "Lazarus, come out!" The dead man came out, his hands and feet bound with strips of cloth, and his face wrapped in a cloth. Jesus said to them, "Unbind him and let him go."

Many of the Jews therefore, who had come with Mary and had seen what Jesus did, believed in him. But some of them went to the Pharisees and told them what he had done.[162]

Comments

We met Mary and Martha earlier, in the story recorded in the Gospel of Luke, but their brother, Lazarus, was not a part of that story (see Chapter 11 of this book). Some details in the two stories are the same. Jesus is a friend of this family and possibly a frequent guest. The tension between

---

[162]   Op. cit., *NRSV,* John 11:3–46, pp. 104–105.

the two sisters, which was so evident in Luke, is missing in this account. When Jesus finally arrives in Bethany, both sisters greet him with the same expression: "Lord, if you had been here, my brother would not have died." Their disappointment is overshadowed by their certainty that Jesus could have done something to prevent Lazarus' death. Martha suggests it is not too late for Jesus to act. Mary shows her grief more than Martha.

This long and detailed story is best understood by careful examination of each segment so that we can discover and discuss its richness. Let's start with the beginning:

> Now, a certain man was ill, Lazarus of Bethany, the village of Mary and her sister Martha.

> So the sisters sent a message to Jesus, "Lord, he whom you love is ill." But when Jesus heard it, he said, "This illness does not lead to death, rather it is for God's glory, so that the Son of God may be glorified through it." Accordingly, though Jesus loved Martha and her sister and Lazarus, after having heard that Lazarus was ill, he stayed two days longer in the place where he was.[163]

When their brother, Lazarus, becomes ill, the sisters take the initiative. The message they deliver to Jesus asserts that Jesus loves their brother, and they urge Jesus to come immediately to assist in his healing and save his life. John lets us know that Jesus deliberately chooses to wait, to not go to Lazarus and his sisters when he is first advised of his friend's illness. Instead, he claims that Lazarus' illness will demonstrate God's glory and will glorify Jesus as God's son. The disciples do not appear to understand that statement by Jesus. Two days pass before Jesus declares that he is ready to set out for Bethany.

---

[163] Ibid., *NRSV,* John 11:3–6, p. 10.

Guided Meditation

Imagine how Jesus's delay affects the sisters.

Apparently, Jesus is allowing his friend to die and the sisters to suffer in order to promote God's glory. Is this hard for you to understand?

The Next Segment of the Story

> Then after this [Jesus] said to the disciples, "Let us go to Judea again." The disciples said to him, "Rabbi, the Jews were just now trying to stone you, and are you going there again?" Jesus answered, "Are there not twelve hours of daylight? Those who walk during the day do not stumble, because they see the light of this world. But those who walk at night stumble, because the light is not in them." After saying this, he told them, "Our friend Lazarus has fallen asleep, but I am going there to awaken him." The disciples said to him, "Lord, if he has fallen asleep, he will be all right." Jesus, however, had been speaking about his death, but they thought that he was referring merely to sleep. Then Jesus told them plainly, "Lazarus is dead. For your sake I am glad I was not there, so that you may believe. But let us go to him." Thomas who was called the Twin, said to his fellow disciples, "Let us go, that we may die with him."[164]

---

[164] Ibid., *NRSV,* John 11:7–16, p. 104.

Comments

When Jesus informs his disciples that they must go to Lazarus, they question his judgment, indicating that he shouldn't go back to a place where he has been threatened. The answer Jesus gives sounds puzzling: he compares walking by day where there is light to walking at night when it is difficult to see the way. Implicit is the notion that safety is provided by the light of God, whereas those in the dark, without God, will be unsafe and stumble.

When Jesus speaks of Lazarus again, his words continue to be confusing to the disciples. Lazarus, he says, "has fallen asleep." When they interpret his comment literally, they miss his meaning. John is showing us that Jesus uses figures of speech that the disciples are unable to comprehend. If Lazarus has just fallen asleep, they conclude, he will be all right, and if that is so, they see no need to endanger themselves. Their failure to understand forces Jesus to be more explicit. "Lazarus is dead," he explains. He then says that the opportunity has been set for them to believe in the power of God that flows through him. I think when Thomas suggests that they all should die as well that the story is demonstrating their failure to understand Jesus.

The Next Segment of the Story

> When Jesus arrived, he found that Lazarus had already been in the tomb four days. Now Bethany was near Jerusalem, some two miles away, and many of the Jews had come to Martha and Mary to console them about their brother. When Martha heard that Jesus was coming, she went out to meet him, while Mary stayed at home.[165]

The stage is set. Lazarus has been dead four days, long enough for decay to set in. The mourners have come to the house, which is customary.

---

[165]   Ibid., NRSV, John 11:17–20, p. 105.

Before Jesus and his disciples arrive at the house, Martha goes out to meet Jesus in order to speak with him privately:

> Martha said to Jesus, "Lord, if you had been here, my brother would not have died. But even now I know that God will give you whatever you ask of him." Jesus said to her, "Your brother will rise again." Martha said to him, "I know that he will rise again in the resurrection on the last day." Jesus said to her, "I am the resurrection and the life. Those who believe in me, even though they die, will live, and everyone who lives and believes in me, will never die. Do you believe this?" She said to him, "Yes, Lord, I believe that you are the Messiah, the Son of God, the one coming into the world."[166]

Comments

Martha confronts Jesus. With an impassioned and accusatory tone, she says, "If you had been here, my brother would not have died." But she doesn't stop there. She goads him with the words, "Even now I know that God will give you whatever you ask." She wants him to act.

Jesus stops her by saying, "Your brother will rise again." This promise is said with certainty; his tone is emphatic. But Martha misunderstands and confirms what is generally believed by saying, "I know that he will rise again in the resurrection on the last day." Belief in a final resurrection is a strong component of Pharisaic Judaism.[167] But Martha is not stating what Jesus means, which leads him to be even bolder in affirming who he is. He states, "I am the resurrection and the life. Those who believe in me, even though they die, will live, and everyone who lives and believes in me will never die."[168]

---

[166] Ibid., *NRSV*, John 11:21–27, p. 105.

[167] Op. cit., Barrett, p. 395.

[168] Op. cit., *NRSV*, John 11:25b–26a, p. 105.

This assertion by Jesus is the strongest self-revelation that he has ever uttered: "I am the resurrection and the life; those who believe in me, even though they die, will live, and everyone who lives and believes in me will never die." Jesus is saying that resurrection is not just a victory over death, he is saying that *he* is a life-giving force for all who believe he is "the Messiah, the Son of God."[169] And then Jesus turns to Martha and asks her whether she believes this. And this strong woman and beloved friend is given the opportunity to profess her faith in who Jesus is. What she says is the same as Peter's assertion in the Gospel of Matthew.[170] Elisabeth Moltmann-Wendel, one of the first to look at the women around Jesus, notes that, in the early Church, "to confess Christ in this way was the mark of an apostle."[171] It makes me wonder why Peter's confession of faith led Jesus to name him as the founder of the church—why not Martha?

The Next Segment of the Story

Just as women were the first witnesses of the Risen Lord, Martha is the first to learn that Jesus is the resurrection. This is the first climax of this story. In this segment, Martha is active, assertive, and quick. But it does not end here. Martha goes back and talks privately with her sister Mary. Because she wants Mary to approach Jesus, she tells her that Jesus is calling for her, even though he was not:

> "The Teacher is here and is calling for you." And when
> she heard it, she got up quickly and went to him. Now
> Jesus had not yet come to the village, but was still at the
> place where Martha had met him. The Jews who were with
> her in the house, consoling her, saw Mary get up quickly
> and go out. They followed her because they thought that
> she was going to the tomb to weep there. When Mary
> came to where Jesus was, she knelt at his feet and said to

---

[169] Flanagan, Neal M. *The Gospel According to John and the Johannine Epistles*, pp 52–52. Flanagan adds: "One who has faith, even after death, shall live; one who has faith and is alive will never really die."

[170] Op. cit., *NRSV*, Matthew16:6, p. 18.

[171] Elisabeth Moltmann-Wendel, *The Women Around Jesus*, p. 25.

him, "Lord, had you been here, my brother would not have died." When Jesus saw her weeping, and the Jews who came with her also weeping, he was greatly disturbed in spirit and deeply moved. He said, "Where have you laid him?" They said to him, "Lord, come and see." Jesus began to weep. So the Jews said, "See how he loved him!" But some of them said, "Could not he who opened the eyes of the blind man have kept this man from dying?"[172]

Mary approaches Jesus because she believes he has called for her. She kneels at his feet as a supplicant and is unable to withhold her tears or her sorrow. She says bluntly that if Jesus had come sooner, her brother need not have died. Seeing Mary weep, Jesus also weeps. He may be deeply moved by Mary's sorrow, similar to the pity he expressed for the widow from Nain, or as some commentators suggest, Jesus's grief may be a response to the unbelief of Mary and her Jewish comforters shown by their weeping.[173]

Reflection Question

When you hear that Jesus wept, what is your reaction?

The Final Segments of the Story

Then Jesus, again gravely disturbed, came to the tomb. It was a cave, and a stone was lying against it. Jesus said, "Take away the stone." Martha, the sister of the dead man, said to him, "Lord, already there is a stench because he has

---

[172] Op. cit., *NRSV*, John 11:28b–37, p. 105.
[173] Op. cit., Barrett, p. 400.

163

been dead four days." Jesus said to her, "Did I not tell you
that if you believed, you would see the glory of God?"[174]

Martha's objection is practical, she is concerned with the stench of the
corpse because she believes that Lazarus is dead. Her objection also shows
that she does not comprehend Jesus's promise. Having not yet experienced
resurrection, it is not real for her until Lazarus actually appears, covered
by his burial wrappings. Her objection gives Jesus another opportunity to
proclaim his intent to reveal God's glory and his own.

> So they took away the stone. And Jesus looked upward
> and said, "[God] I thank you for having heard me. I knew
> that you always hear me, but I have said this for the sake
> of the crowd standing here, so that they may believe that
> you sent me."[175]

Here, we see the reliance of Jesus on God to perform extraordinary deeds
and his confidence that his prayers will be answered. Jesus is certain that
God will be seen in and through the works of Jesus.

> When he said this, he cried with a loud voice, "Lazarus,
> come out!" The dead man came out, his hands and feet
> bound with strips of cloth, and his face wrapped in a
> cloth. Jesus said to them, "Unbind him and let him go."[176]

> Many of the Jews, who had come with Mary and
> had seen what Jesus did, believed in him. But some of
> them went to the Pharisees and told them what he had
> done.[177]

---

[174] Op. cit., *NRSV*, John 11: 38–40, p. 105.
[175] Ibid., *NRSV*, John 11:41–42, p. 105.
[176] Ibid., *NRSV*, John 11:43–44, p. 105.
[177] Ibid., *NRSV*, John 11:45–46, p. 105.

Lazarus responds to the sound of Jesus's voice like a sheep who knows the voice of his shepherd. Wrapped in the cloths of burial, Lazarus comes out alive.[178] This is a fulfillment of the earlier promise that Jesus made, which appears in the fifth Chapter of the Gospel of John:

> "Very truly, I tell you, the hour is coming, and is now here, when the dead will hear the voice of the Son of God, and those who hear will live."[179]

Guided Meditation

Have you ever wondered how Lazarus felt about being brought back to life? Imagine what Lazarus was feeling as he emerged from the cave.

Just imagine the sisters' excitement when they witnessed this miracle! Their sorrow and their resentment are transformed.

Conclusions

To be an eye witness to this event had two different effects: some observers became believers, and some saw evidence that the Pharisees could use against Jesus. This miracle galvanized Jesus's enemies to arrest, try, and crucify him.

The story is a reminder to all of us that God does not always answer our prayers as soon as or how we might wish.

---

[178] Op. cit., Barrett, p. 388.
[179] Ibid., *NRSV*, John 5:25, p. 96.

There are striking differences in how Martha and Mary are portrayed by Luke and John.[180] Luke's description shows the sisters in conflict because Martha is annoyed that Mary is listening to Jesus and not helping her. That story continues to generate issues regarding appropriate roles for women. John's Martha is more attractive to the independent woman of today: she is self-aware, forthright, and persistent. She transcends the traditional feminine role. Mary is also forthright; she expresses her feelings and her dashed hope. In John, Mary continues to look like a devoted disciple, one who kneels at Jesus's feet and cries over her loss of Lazarus.

In this story, Martha and Mary are able to witness the glory of God. Jesus's conversations with the sisters change this miracle story about the raising of Lazarus into a story about the new life that is available to those who believe in him. This is the last of the signs reported by John that demonstrate Jesus's power. The story also serves as a precursor to the plot to crucify him.

Final Reflection Question

Regardless of which of the sisters you identified with in the story from Luke, how do you react to John's portrait of Martha and Mary?

---

[180] Ibid., Moltmann-Wendel, p. 27.

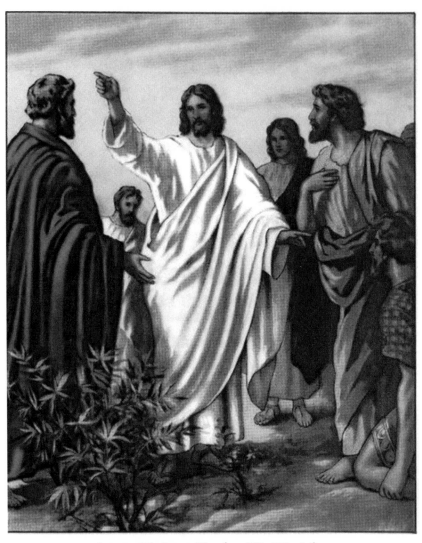

Image 16: Jesus Teaches His Disciples
The First Shall Be Last in the Kingdom

CHAPTER 16:
JESUS ANSWERS
THE MOTHER OF ZEBEDEE'S SONS

James and John were fishermen with Zebedee, their father. On the day that Jesus called Simon Peter and Andrew, he also called the Zebedee brothers when they were returning from a day at sea. They travelled around with Jesus as he taught and healed people, and as a result, they became close to him. Their mother saw how devoted they were to Jesus.

In the Gospel of Mark, Zebedee's sons request a special favor. They ask Jesus to reserve a place for each of them on his right and left side in his glory.[181] At first, Jesus questions them about their readiness to drink from his cup.[182] Acknowledging that they will suffer, Jesus answers that he does not have the power to bestow those honors in God's realm.

Matthew tells an almost identical story, but he places it later in Jesus's ministry and attributes the question to the mother of the sons of Zebedee rather than her sons. There is considerable speculation as to why Matthew modifies the story and shifts responsibility for the request to the mother. None of the evidence that I have seen explains Matthew's changes. Whatever his reasons, Matthew gives us yet another image of a woman who encounters Jesus. This woman is identified by her relationship to the men in her life, like so many of the others.

As the Zebedee brothers go with their mother to meet Jesus, she approaches Jesus as a supplicant. Here is how Matthew describes the incident:

---

[181] Op. cit., *NRSV*, Mark 10:35–45.
[182] Cup is a common synonym for suffering.

Then the mother of the sons of Zebedee came to Jesus with her sons, and kneeling before him, she asked a favor of him. And [Jesus] said to her, "what do you want?" She said to him, "Declare that these two sons of mine will sit, one at your right hand and one at your left, in your [realm]." But Jesus answered, "You do not know what you are asking. Are you able to drink the cup that I am about to drink?" They said to him, "We are able." He said to them, "You will indeed drink my cup, but to sit at my right hand and at my left, this is not mine to grant, but it is for those for whom it has been prepared by [God]."

When the other disciples heard this, they were angry with the two brothers. But Jesus called them to him and said, "You know that the rulers of the Gentiles lord it over them. It will not be so among you, but whoever wishes to be great among you must be your servant, and whoever wishes to be first among you must be your slave. Just as the Son of [Humanity] came not to be served but to serve, and to give his life a ransom for many."[183]

Guided Meditation

In Matthew's account of this incident, the mother is asking for something for her sons, not for herself. Imagine how proud she is of them and how much she wants the best for them.

---

[183] Op. cit., *NRSV*, Matthew 20:20-28, p. 22.

Because her sons have spent three years engaged in Jesus's ministry, she asks for something in return. Imagine her desire for Jesus to assure her that they will have an important and prominent place in his realm.

Comments

Jewish women were respected if they were mothers, especially those who were mothers of sons. Most mothers saw their whole worth embodied in their sons.[184] Most likely, she is assuming that, if her sons are honored, she will be honored as their mother. Hopes for a Messiah made childless women despair and inspired hope in pregnant women.

As a mother, her willingness to make an effort for the sake of her sons is admirable, even if she misunderstands the nature of the realm of Jesus. She does not understand that his realm is not of this world.

Jesus listens to her, but when he responds, he speaks directly to her sons. It's as if she hadn't spoken. Like Mark's version of the story, Jesus questions the brothers' readiness to share his cup and suffer. They readily say that they are willing, and Jesus concurs that they will suffer. After that, Jesus explains that it is not his right to choose who will sit by him in God's realm.

Note that the other disciples become angry with James and John, not with their mother.[185] The incident provides Jesus with an opportunity to improve their understanding of a servant-community.

---

[184] Op. cit., Moltmann-Wendel, p. 126.

[185] Douglas R. A. Hare, *Interpretation, A Bible Commentary for Teaching and Preaching: Matthew*, p. 233.

Reflection Questions

Why do you suppose Matthew shifts the maker of the request from the sons, as it appears in Mark, to their mother?

Have there been times when you have asked for favors for your children or your relatives' children? Why? What happened?

Who do you think really initiated this request for a favor, the sons or their mother?

Comments

The requested favor may have been prompted by the assertion of Jesus that once he was seated on the throne of his glory, his twelve disciples would sit on twelve thrones to preside over the twelve tribes of Israel, as recorded in Matthew 19:28. Jesus was surrounded by people who expected him to restore Israel as an independent kingdom.[186] Until their hopes for a messianic reign over Israel were destroyed by the crucifixion of Jesus, some of his disciples probably expected significant roles in his future reign.

In response to these struggles for preferential treatment among his disciples, Jesus announces a revision of power relationships among his followers, so that the customary hierarchy is turned upside down—the last become first and the first become last.[187] Jesus explains that God's reign is not like Caesar's. He turns to all of his disciples and says, "I am among you as one who serves."[188]

In speaking of his future realm, Jesus often compares tyranny and servanthood as a sign that his will be a community that is open to all, not just rich and poor, but also the oppressed, the outcasts, the sick, the prisoners, and the women and children.

These stories of the women Jesus encountered have convinced me that Jesus offers us a vision of a new world where even women have a place of respect, where there is enough food for everyone and no one has power over others.

---

[186] Op. cit., Hare, pp. 232–233.
[187] Op. cit., *NRSV*, Matthew 20:27 p. 22.
[188] Op. cit., *NRSV*, Matthew 20:28 p. 22.

Reflection Questions

Imagine hearing about Jesus's ideas for the first time. How do you react?

Jesus describes the new order he hopes to establish. How close have we come to that vision? Is it still your hope for the future?

Conclusions

Matthew is the only Gospel writer who reports that the mother of Zebedee's sons was included with the group of women present at the crucifixion of Jesus, which suggests that she joined her sons as they traveled with Jesus (after learning the lessons of discipleship).[189] I find it ironic that, when Jesus is crucified, she risks arrest by being present with the other women at the Cross, while her sons hide in fear.

---

[189]   Op. cit., Binz, p. 68.

Mothers of today can learn from the mother of James and John— regarding both motherhood and discipleship. This story is a reminder to all of us: even if we offer distinguished service to humanity and the Church, we should not think of ourselves as superior. Our sole goal must be to serve faithfully and express our best effort.

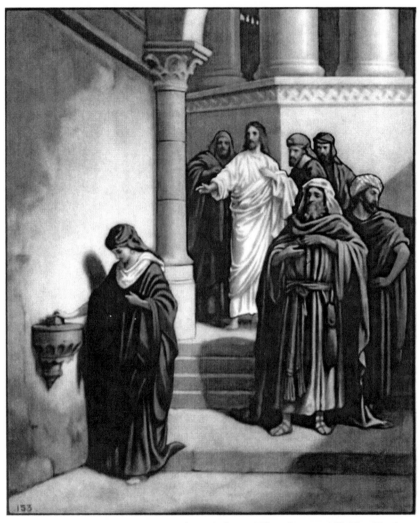

Image 17: Jesus Points to the Widow Who Game All She Had

CHAPTER 17:
JESUS'S COMMENTS ABOUT THE POOR WIDOW

The story of the generosity of a poor widow is as much of a challenge to our own materialistic, status-seeking society as it was to the world of Jesus. On his third visit to the Temple in the week before his death, Jesus compares the ostentatious generosity of the influential, rich people with the genuine piety of a poor widow.

This brief story is situated between Jesus's debates with the Temple leadership (Mark 11:27–12:40) and his final teaching with his disciples about the Temple's future destruction.[190] In the segment in Mark that appears just prior to this story, Jesus criticizes the religious leaders who parade around pursuing admiration and looking for positions of prominence on public occasions.[191]

Mark tells us that Jesus sat down opposite the Temple treasury and watched the crowd putting money into the treasury. Many rich people put in large sums so that others would notice.[192] In contrast, Mark reports the following:

> A poor widow came and put in two small copper coins, which are worth a penny. Then [Jesus] called his disciples and said to them, "Truly I tell you, this poor widow has put in more than all those who are contributing to the treasury. For all of them have contributed out of

---

[190] Smith, Dennis E. and Michael E. Williams (Eds.), *The Storyteller's Companion to the Bible, Volume Thirteen: New Testament Women*, p. 79.

[191] Kalas, J. Ellsworth, *Strong Was Her Faith*, p. 50.

[192] Op. cit., *NRSV*, Mark 12: 41, p. 50.

their abundance; but she out of her poverty has put in everything she had, all that she had to live on."[193]

Her two coins made up the smallest unit of money at that time. Since she only has two coins, the widow is giving all that she has. Eugene Peterson's description of this scene in Mark enables us to appreciate fully the gist of Jesus's remarks:

> One poor widow came up and put in two small coins—a measly two cents. Jesus called the disciples over and said, "The truth is that this poor widow gave more to the collection than all the others put together. All the others gave what they'll never miss, she gave extravagantly what she couldn't afford—she gave her all."[194]

Guided Meditation

Imagine the widow approaching the treasury with her two small coins. She knows that this isn't a large amount of money, but it is all she has. She is giving her all.

Imagine her gratitude for all that God has given her.

---

[193] Ibid., *NRSV*, MARK 12:42–44, P. 50. This story also appears in Luke 21:1–4, p. 85.
[194] Op. cit., *MSG*, Mark 12: 41–44, p. 1849.

Imagine Jesus as he sits and watches the ostentatious donations of the other givers. Suddenly, he sees the widow. Imagine his response as he sees the extent of her generosity.

Reflection Questions

Do you think the widow was aware that Jesus was talking about her and using her as an example for his disciples?

Why, after all these years, do you think she is still remembered?

Identify a time when someone who appeared to be more needy than you (emotionally, spiritually, physically, or financially) was very generous to you and write about it here.

Think of an occasion when you were truly generous in ways unique to you and write about it.

On many occasions, Jesus cites the exemplary behavior of a believer. Often, he discusses that person's generosity in terms of giving money and sharing possessions. How might your giving be more like the poor widow's?

Do you see the widow's self-sacrifice as a precursor to Jesus's passion? Why or why not?

Conclusions

As noted earlier in this book, when a woman lost her husband, she lost her sole source of financial support and protection. Whereas some were able to rely on other family members and in-laws, poor widows were often left destitute.[195] Throughout the Hebrew Scriptures, "widows are the special object of God's concern."[196] Israel is warned not to treat widows unjustly.[197]

The Jewish tradition emphasizes a form of social justice that requires them to care for the poor, but Gentile believers who were the recipients of Mark's Gospel lacked that tradition.[198] With this story, Mark shows that Jesus wanted his disciples to notice that the widow's poverty and insecurity did not limit her generosity. Grateful for how richly God had blessed her, she demonstrated that she trusted that God would see the fullness of her heart and accept whatever she had to offer.[199]

When the widow gave everything she had as her contribution to the welfare of others, it was an act of extreme generosity, an act of great self-sacrifice, and an act of total reliance on God.[200]

---

[195] Op. cit., Smith and Williams (Eds.), p. 79.

[196] Op. cit., Thurston, p. 74.

[197] See, e.g., Exodus 22:22–24; Deuteronomy 24:17, 27:19 and Jeremiah 22:3.

[198] Op. cit., Getty-Sullivan, pp. 206–207.

[199] Op. cit., Binz, p. 132.

[200] Op. cit., Swidler, pp. 61–62.

Jesus observes her, but he does not speak to her directly; he uses her as an example to teach the others.

By calling his disciples over and speaking to them about the widow's generosity, Jesus's comments form an important teaching for the church—then and now. The woman's action is worthy of praise because she gives despite her poverty, and she does so without reservation or self-protection.

One of the most important lessons that Jesus teaches has to do with intentionality: what is important about a human being is his or her intention (*kavod* in Hebrew).[201] The widow's gift is illustrative of a wholehearted commitment to God that is similar to the one Jesus is about to make in giving up his own life. Her gift is a model for all of us who think of ourselves as disciples.

True generosity, giving with no strings attached or expectations of a return, is truly a gift of grace. That grace comes from God and is a response to the enormity of God's grace.

Many commentators are uncomfortable with Jesus's praise for the poor widow. Smith and Williams note that the Temple, as a "place of redistribution of tithes and taxes, should have been providing the sustenance that the poor widow needed, instead of taking it from her.[202] Binz concludes that "like the sacrificial offering of Jesus on the cross, the woman's gift is both an injustice and a selfless offering, which is both lamentable and commendable like the crucifixion that follows."[203] Thurston and other writers suggest that Jesus's praise of her generosity should have been a lament over a religious institution that would lead such a person to give away all she has. Given its size, this woman's gift actually did not contribute to those who were destitute. Smith and Williams add that it merely contributes to a corrupt system that devours the resources

---

[201]

[202] Op cit, Smith and Williams (Eds.), p. 80.
[203] Op. cit., Binz, p. 133.

of poor widows.[204] Jesus, like the prophet Jeremiah, was critical of the Temple redistribution process. In the next chapter of Mark, he predicts the destruction of the Temple.[205]

Many of these writers see the woman's offering as a preface to Jesus's own offering for the salvation of humanity. Often, this virtue of sacrificial giving has led to a woman's negation of herself and a codependent view of her relationship with others. It is as if her identity is embedded in others. Christian churches need to teach both self-care *and* self-sacrifice!

This story is a good example of a story that has been preserved because it reveals "what is valued and sacred to a community."[206] The widow's gesture displayed a generous heart, which is the essential expression of true faith.

204   Op. cit., *NRSV,* Mark 12:40, p. 49, cited by Smith and Williams, p. 80.

205   Ibid., *NRSV,* Mark 13:2, p. 50.

206   Op. cit., Pearson, p. 14.

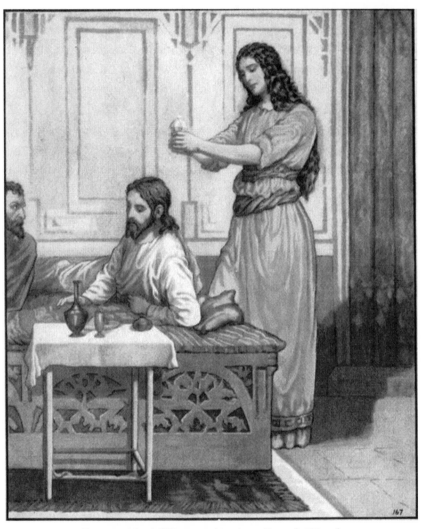

Image 18: A Woman Anoints Jesus's Head

CHAPTER 18:
A WOMAN ANOINTS JESUS
BEFORE HIS DEATH

All four Gospels describe a woman anointing Jesus. In the stories of the Hebrew Bible, prophets are anointed as a way of recognizing that their authority comes from God. Similarly, priests and kings are anointed to show their authority is recognized as God given. The term, *Messiah* means *The Anointed One*. When the woman anoints the head of Jesus, her action signifies her acceptance of Jesus as "The Anointed One, the Messiah."[207]

The praise that Jesus expresses for this woman is remembered. Like the poor widow at the Temple, she offers the disciples of Jesus an example of generous loving. At a time when his male disciples are unable or unwilling to grasp the prospect of his imminent death, Jesus acknowledges that this woman is preparing him for his burial. By courageously ministering to Jesus, she replicates the compassionate behavior of Jesus. Clearly, Jesus appreciates this woman's actions. She gives to him without any expectation of reciprocity. Her actions are still being recalled and praised just as the actions of Jesus are praised.

Though unnamed, the woman's activities lead Pearson, author of *Do What You Have the POWER to Do*, to say that she serves "as an example of a true disciple of Jesus" because "she does what she has the power to do."[208]

Although the Gospels are unanimous that this incident happened, their portrayals vary *greatly*. In Mark and Matthew's stories, she is unnamed and

---

[207] Op. cit., Getty-Sullivan, p. 216.
[208] Op. cit., Pearson, p. 37.

185

anoints Jesus's head. John identifies the woman as Mary of Bethany, the sister of Lazarus. In addition to providing dinner at their home, she anoints the feet of Jesus. In Luke, she is labeled a forgiven sinner who anoints his feet in gratitude.

The Gospels of Mark and Matthew

Mark and Matthew's event occurs two days before the celebration of the Passover. Their accounts are almost identical. Mark says:

> While [Jesus] was at Bethany at the home of Simon the Leper, as he sat at table, a woman came with an alabaster jar of very costly ointment of nard and she broke open the jar and poured the ointment on the head of Jesus.
>
> But some were there who said to one another in anger, "why was the ointment wasted in this way? For this ointment could have been sold for more than three hundred denarii, and the money given to the poor." And they scolded her. But Jesus said, "Let her alone; why do you trouble her? She has performed a good service for me. For you always have the poor with you, and you can show kindness to them whenever you wish; but you will not always have me. She has done what she could; she has anointed my body beforehand for its burial. Truly I tell you, wherever the good news is proclaimed in the whole world, what she has done will be told in remembrance of her."[209]

Comments

There are four important details within this shared account: first, the woman is unnamed; second, the home of Simon the leper in Bethany is where the anointing takes place; third, it is the *head* of Jesus that is

---

[209]   Op. cit., *NRSV*, Mark 14:3–9, p. 51.

anointed; and fourth, the event takes place just before the crucifixion of Jesus, and it is interpreted by Jesus as preparation for his burial.[210]

Mark and Matthew tell us nothing about who this woman is. We know that she is unafraid and bold, and that she treats Jesus with tenderness and compassion.

Many scholars report how unusual this event is. Banquet hosts often anointed the heads of their guests to express hospitality and provide refreshment, but Simon does not do that.[211] Pearson adds that "to anoint the head of a designated leader of the people was considered a prophetic activity" that was not a woman's task. But it is not Simon or the male guests and disciples who anoint Jesus; it is a woman who is "acting, caring, touching, anointing, giving and risking."[212]

Her actions are extraordinary: she bursts into a dinner where the invited guests are *all* male. And then she breaks open an alabaster jar of perfumed ointment and anoints the head of Jesus with *all* of its contents. By anointing Jesus, she assumes the male role of both the host and the one selected to anoint a king.

These are acts of consecration of a Messiah and of preparation for his burial. Without saying a word, her message is as follows: "This is The Anointed One! This is the Messiah!"[213] Restricted to silence in the company of men, she answers the question of who Jesus is by her action of anointing him Messiah.

Moltmann-Wendel emphasizes this linkage when she states that this "unknown woman is at the same time a prophet who anoints the Messiah, consecrates him and prepares him for his task" ahead,[214] just as the prophet

---

210   Cynthia Bourgeault, p. 18.
211   Op. cit., Binz, p. 137.
212   Op. cit., Pearson, p. 47.
213   Ibid., Pearson, p. 42.
214   Op. cit., Moltmann-Wendel, p.98.

Samuel anointed Saul and later David. [215] Pearson adds that "to anoint the head of a designated leader of the people was considered a prophetic activity," which is not a woman's task.[216]

Moltmann-Wendel also notes that, in Mark, Jesus is "more of a human being and more physical than in the other Gospels: "He enjoys the gesture of anointing, trembles in anguish in Gethsemane and dies with an inarticulate cry."[217]

Guided Meditation

Imagine this bold and courageous woman who entered a room full of men with the purpose of anointing the head of Jesus.

Imagine Jesus brooding over the events that are about to happen in Jerusalem when this woman beaks open her alabaster jar ands pours its contents over his head.

---

[215]   Ibid., Moltmann-Wendel, p. 98.

[216]   Ibid., Pearson, p. 42.

[217]   Ibid., Moltmann-Wendel, p. 102.

<u>Reflection Questions</u>

If her deeds were so remarkable and forever remembered, why do you think her name was not remembered?

This unnamed woman's story of offering Jesus comfort before his impending death is more important than the stories of the named persons who betrayed Jesus and denied knowing him. Why aren't her actions better known?

Think about yourself. Are you willing to do something unexpected for Jesus? What might that be?

Comments

This anointing of Jesus takes place two days before the Jewish feast of the Passover, after Jesus arrives in Jerusalem. At the same time, there are those in Jerusalem who are so threatened by the popularity of Jesus that they begin looking for a way to arrest and kill him. The openly daring and excessive behavior of this woman is a sharp contrast to the secret maneuvers of the religious authorities to arrest and kill Jesus.

Of all the women who encountered Jesus, she is the only one of whom Jesus says, "Truly I tell you, wherever the good news is proclaimed in the whole world, what she has done will be told in remembrance of her."[218]

"Jesus praises her deed more highly than he praised any other deed in the Gospel."[219] Even after two thousand years, she remains a model for us, reminding us to do what we have the power to do.

The Anointing Woman in the Gospel of John

If the stories that appear in Mark and Matthew were the only Gospel accounts of a woman anointing Jesus, these early accounts would be interpreted as Jesus appears to understand them. However, there are two other gospel stories of an anointing woman that differ from the ones found in Mark and Matthew.

The Gospel of John follows the same plotline as seen in Mathew and Mark. However, John places this event at the home of Jesus's friend, Lazarus, in Bethany. He names the woman who does the anointing, Mary of Bethany, the sister of Lazaarus. This event also occurs before the crucifixion, and it is seen as a preparation for his burial. The anointing stories that appear in Mark, Matthew, and John bear so many similarities that many regard them as the same story. However, the anointing of Jesus's *feet* in John's Gospel has no Messianic implications.

---

[218] Op cit, *NRSV*, Mark 14:9, p. 51
[219] Op. cit., Binz, p. 138

In John, the female figure is Mary, the sister whom Jesus praised for listening attentively to him earlier. This family is shown throughout John's Gospel to be special friends of Jesus; therefore, another dinner in Bethany with them is not unlikely and fits John's interest in this family. John's account also includes Jesus's praise for Mary's actions. As John tells it[220]:

> Six days before the Passover, Jesus came to Bethany, the home of Lazarus, whom he had raised from the dead. There they gave a dinner for him. Martha served and Lazarus was one of those at the table with him. Mary took a pound of costly perfume made of pure nard, anointed Jesus's feet, and wiped them with her hair. The house was filled with the fragrance of the perfume. But Judas Iscariot, one of his disciples (the one who was about to betray him), said, "Why was this perfume not sold for three hundred denarii and the money given to the poor?" (He said this not because he cared about the poor, but because he was a thief; he kept the common purse and used to steal what was put into it.) Jesus said, "Leave her alone. She bought it so that she might keep it for the day of my burial. You always have the poor with you but you do not always have me."

Again, there is no sign that the disciples understand or expect Jesus to die an untimely death. On three different occasions in the Gospel of John, Jesus tells his disciples that he will suffer and die, but they see him as invincible. They cannot imagine that their revolution will end with his suffering and death.

Only Mary of Bethany appears to be aware that Jesus's death is imminent. Her behavior in this version of the story is also extravagant. The perfume she uses is costly, equal to a year's wages at that time. The scent is so fragrant that it fills the room. Here, it is Judas who complains about the waste; he does not rejoice in her act of generosity. This is Mary's way of showing her love. But Jesus does not seem embarrassed by Mary's

---

220   Op. cit., *NRSV*, John 12:1-8, p. 107

exuberant conduct. Rather than finding it inappropriate, he sees the gift as preparation for his burial."[221]

Comments on Preparation for Death

The woman's actions are a reminder that the dying need companionship and comfort. Some people can talk about the path to death, but many cannot. Being there is a blessing for both of you. In our far-flung nation and world, a website called Caring Bridge allows friends and family to stay connected with critically ill people to comfort them.

Reflection Questions

Have you ever been extravagant in the way that you displayed your love? What did you do? What prompted you to do that?

Have you ever been at the bedside of someone close to you who was dying? What did you say or do? How was that experience?

---

[221] Op. cit., Getty-Sullivan, p. 219

The Anointing Woman in the Gospel of Luke

Luke changes the story in dramatic ways.[222] The banquet takes place at the home of a Pharisee earlier in Jesus's ministry in Galilee. Thus, it is unrelated to any preparation for the death and crucifixion of Jesus.

The unnamed woman in Luke's Gospel is one who was known as a sinner. Since the towns were small, we can assume that everybody knew everybody. This woman came into the house not seeking forgiveness, but recognizing that forgiveness had already been granted to her. The event's meaning is conveyed in the following principle: "The one who is forgiven more loves more."

The actions of the unnamed woman in Luke's Gospel are also lavish and effusive. Typically, the one who has been pardoned falls at the feet of the one granting pardon and kisses that person's feet. By weeping and kneeling at the feet of Jesus, washing them with her tears, wiping them with her hair, and kissing them and anointing them with extravagant perfume, she is showing signs of her love and gratitude for being pardoned previously. When complaints are raised about her lavish behavior, Jesus compares her hospitality to the lack of hospitality shown by his host:

> "Do you see this woman? I entered your house; you gave me no water for my feet, but she has bathed my feet with her tears and dried them with her hair. You gave me no kiss but from the time I came in she has not stopped kissing my feet. You did not anoint my head with oil, but she has anointed my feet with ointment. Therefore, I tell you, her sins, which were many, have been forgiven; hence she has shown great love. But the one to whom little is forgiven, loves little."[223]

---

[222] Op. cit., Getty-Sullivan, p. 213
[223] Op. cit., *NRSV*, Luke 7:44b–47, p. 66.

Then he said to her, "Your sins are forgiven."[224]

And he said to the woman, "Your faith has saved you; go in peace."[225]

Comments on Luke's Story

Before Jesus's ministry, a sinner in Hebrew circles was believed to live and die a sinner. So this woman's gratitude over being forgiven is genuine and has been an inspiration to other sinners throughout the last two thousand years, despite the source of their sin.

The Pharisees were authoritative in the interpretation of the Law. They held strict ideas about the holy and the unclean and did not associate with sinners. The story corresponds with the accusation in Luke that Jesus is a friend of tax collectors and sinners.[226]

Simon the Pharisee fails to recognize and correctly interpret the woman's actions as well as Jesus's role in her forgiveness. He assumes that if Jesus were really a prophet, he would have recognized the woman as a sinner and scorned her. Because Jesus recognizes that she has been forgiven and is lavishly showing her appreciation, he compares her to Simon. Implicit is the notion that Simon has not known forgiveness or knows no need for forgiveness and loves little by comparison.

The first words spoken by Jesus to this woman affirm her conviction that she has been forgiven. He is appreciative of her gratitude and accepting of her, despite her past. His response is a reflection of the magnanimity of God's love toward all people. Jesus not only speaks to her, he allows her to touch him and kiss him.

---

[224] Ibid., *NRSV,* Luke 7:48, pp. 66–67.

[225] Ibid., *NRSV,* Luke 7:50, pp. 67.

[226] Op. cit., *NRSV,* Luke 7:34, p. 66.

A woman was not allowed to let her hair be uncovered, and to unloose it in public was grounds for divorce. Yet this woman uncovers her hair, loosens it, and wipes Jesus's feet with it. In response, Jesus rebukes the Pharisee and welcomes the woman and her actions. The others seated at the same table recognize that she is forgiven, and they ask themselves, "Who is this who even forgives sins?"[227] Like the woman healed of a hemorrhage, Jesus tells her that her" faith saved her; go in peace.'[228]

Guided Meditation

Look at this story from the vantage point of the woman who has been forgiven. She does not appear uncomfortable intruding the banquet uninvited.

Notice that, even though her actions are dramatic and intentional, she is gentle and loving.

Imagine what she may be saying to herself to assure herself of her worth in the presence of all those men.

---

[227] Ibid., *NRSV,* Luke 7:50b, p. 67.
[228] Ibid., *NRSV,* Luke 7:50b, p. 67.

Now look at Jesus. He watches her carefully and recognizes that she is acting this way to express her gratitude for being forgiven. His face softens as he observes her and experiences her loving gestures.

Imagine how this woman reacts to Jesus when he affirms her actions.

Comments

Because this woman is called a sinner, many interpreters have called her a prostitute, although the text does not explicitly make this connection. Given the male tendency to see women as sexually seductive and immoral, the prostitute label has persisted even though there is no textual foundation for it.

We need to remember her as a forgiven woman whose appreciation is great, whatever the source of her sin. Once forgiven, the nature of her sin is irrelevant. She is now transformed into a person whose gratitude and love inspire her actions and our respect. Luke's purpose in telling this story is clearly different than the other three Gospel writers.

Luke's Gospel is usually dated circa 85 AD, after the destruction of the Temple, when the Pharisees assumed prominence as interpreters of the Law. In the absence of the Temple, the Law became more important.[229] One of the reasons Jesus was rejected was that he did not conform to the expectations of Jewish leaders such as the Pharisees. In Luke's account, the behavior of the inhospitable Pharisee Simon is compared to the hospitality of the anointing woman.

---

[229]   Op. cit., Getty-Sullivan, p. 108.

Getty-Sullivan points out that "the name 'Pharisees' means 'separated or pious ones.'" "They separated themselves from the unrighteous" and the unclean.[230] Because this woman is described as a sinner, Simon challenges Jesus for allowing such a woman to touch him.

Conclusions

All of these stories show that women were not only witnesses but also significant participants in ministry in the first century. As Getty-Sullivan describes them, "They heard the word, they believed, they bore witnesses, they made converts and they had authority."[231]

In each story, the woman is as bold and full of faith as the hemorrhaging woman who touched the hem of Jesus's garment, as clever as the Syro-Phoenician woman who pleaded successfully for her daughter's healing, and as generous as the poor widow who gave her last coins.[232]

What is different in the stories is the purpose of the anointing. In Luke's Gospel, we witness an anointing that expresses the gratitude of the forgiven sinner. In John, we see Mary making preparations for Jesus's death by anointing his feet.

Mark and Mathew present us with an unnamed woman who anoints Jesus's head; her actions are compared to the prophets who anointed kings.

Cynthia Bourgeault, author of *The Meaning of Mary Magdalene*, takes the actions of the two unnamed women in the earliest Gospels to support her belief that the sacramental, unnamed anointer is really Mary Magdalene. She relies on the evidence that both Mary Magdalene and Jesus actually practiced anointing on many occasions, perhaps even as a shared ministry.[233] The reputation of Jesus grew from his actions as a healer and exorcist, and those acts often involved the use of various salves.

---

[230]   Ibid., Getty-Sullivan, p. 108.

[231]   Op. cit., Getty-Sullivan, p. 219.

[232]   Op. cit., Newsom et al, p. 490.

[233]   Op. cit., Bourgeault, p. 183.

For Bourgeault, Jesus's passage through death is framed on both sides by Mary Magdalene's parallel acts of anointing." At Bethany, she sends him to the cross "wearing the unction of her love," and at the tomb "he awakens to the same fragrance."[234] For a fuller description of Cynthia Bourgeault's understanding of Mary Magdalene, see Chapter 20 of this book.

---

[234]   Op. cit., Bourgeault, p. 185.

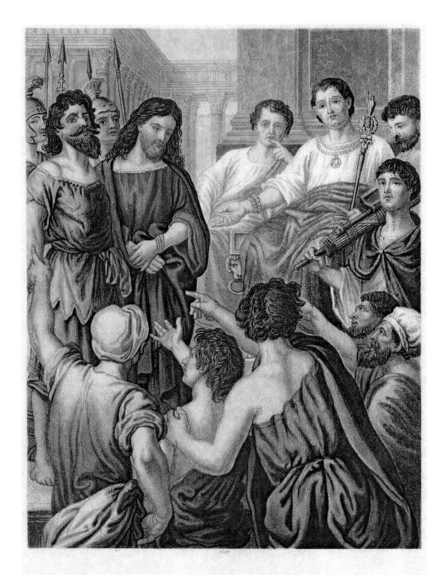

JESUS BEFORE PILATE.

Image 19: Art Depicting Jesus before Pilate

CHAPTER 19:
THE DREAM OF PILATE'S WIFE

In ancient times, dreams were regarded as divine messages warning recipients to take or avoid certain actions. Early in Matthew's Gospel, the Magi were warned in a dream not to return to Herod with news of the Christ child, and another dream led Joseph to flee Herod and escape to Egypt with Mary and their newborn baby. Disturbing dreams were taken seriously in biblical times.[235]

There is a little-known story that only appears in the Gospel of Matthew about Pilate's wife interceding on behalf of Jesus. Just like Joseph and the Magi, she is warned about Jesus in a disturbing dream. As Pilate, the Roman governor, sits listening to Jesus's accusers, trying to determine whether there are sufficient grounds to execute him as the Jewish leaders insist, his wife sends word to him:

> "Have nothing to do with that innocent man, for today I have suffered a great deal because of a dream about him."[236]

Her confidence in the dream gives her a readiness to speak up and have her messenger interrupt the public proceeding. It is likely that the works of Jesus were known to her, although we do not know how she gained that knowledge. Pilate's reluctance to have a role in the execution of Jesus is heightened by his wife's warning. Her dream reveals Jesus to be a righteous man.

---

[235] Op. cit., Swidler, p. 77
[236] Op cit, *NRSV*, Matthew 27:19, p. 32

Guided Meditation

Imagine Pilate's wife awakening from a disturbing dream. Watch her as she replays the events of the dream and ponders its meaning.

Convinced the dream is about Jesus, whom her husband, Pilate, will soon judge, she suddenly gets up out of bed and prepares herself to go out. She is determined to influence Pilate before he decides the fate of Jesus. She knows that, as a woman, she cannot barge in when Pilate sits on the judgment seat, so she asks a servant to deliver the message that she is sure the man is innocent based on a disturbing dream she had about him. Imagine her sense of urgency.

Imagine her returning to their palace to await the outcome of Pilate's decision. She appears apprehensive.

Imagine Pilate as he faces the insistent chief priests and elders of the Temple who are calling for the execution of Jesus before the festival of Passover.

Imagine Pilate turning and listening to his servant's report of his wife's message. Notice that he shakes his head and seems pensive.

As the waiting crowd becomes unruly, imagine Pilate's growing fear that a riot will ensue. Imagine his sense that he must prevent that.

Imagine how Pilate's wife felt when her efforts to save Jesus failed.

Comments

The pagan wife of the Roman governor is not afraid to speak up for Jesus, yet no one else speaks on his behalf. Getty-Sullivan suggests that Pilate's wife seeks to ensure that her report of her suffering will help Pilate take the right action to avoid complicity in Jesus's death.[237] Compare her to Judas, who betrays Jesus; Peter, who denies knowing him; the other disciples, who flee out of fear; and the women, who follow at a distance and weep. The pagan wife's courage and strong convictions are admirable. Still, Pilate is committed to keeping order. Unable to influence the crowds and fearful of an uprising, Pilate is not as courageous as his wife when he turns over Jesus to be crucified.

Reflection Questions

How important are dreams in your life? Do you trust them and the intuitions they inspire?

---

[237] Op. cit., Getty-Sullivan, p. 131-133

If you distrust dreams, why?

What or who do you see to be the source of your dreams?

Have you ever acted on a dream the way Pilate's wife did? What was the outcome?

Are there any dreams or intuitions that you ignored that you now wish you hadn't?

Were there any you followed that you now wish you hadn't?

Are you more or less likely to take your dreams more seriously now that you are aware of the disturbing dream of Pilate's wife?

Conclusions

It appears from Matthew's retelling of the trial that Pilate is not convinced that Jesus is guilty of the crimes raised by the members of the Sanhedrin, but he is unwilling to challenge the insistent mob that has gathered. Many believe that Pilate's failure to listen to his wife may be the worst mistake he ever made.

The dreams of Pilate's wife are central to a dynamic and intriguing novel entitled *Pilate's Wife* by Antoinette May. It provides a vivid portrait of the Roman world in which she and Jesus lived.[238] Described as a woman of privilege in that world's most powerful empire, her marriage to an ambitious magistrate, Pontius Pilate, led her to Judea at a time when the air of open rebellion was very strong. Her dreams are described by May as a unique and disturbing "gift" that have an uncanny way of coming true.

Matthew, however, tells us nothing about Pilate's wife except for her dream. As the wife of the procurator, her lifestyle was Roman, regardless of the location of his assignment. It is likely that something or someone alerted her to the efforts to crucify Jesus, and she cared enough about his innocence to try to influence her husband.

The intervention of Pilate's wife lends a human dimension to the story of Jesus's trial and the subsequent crucifixion that is absent from the other Gospels. If Pilate's wife's actions were given attention, we might view Good Friday differently.

---

[238] May, Antoinette, *Pilate's Wife*. New York: Harper, 2007.

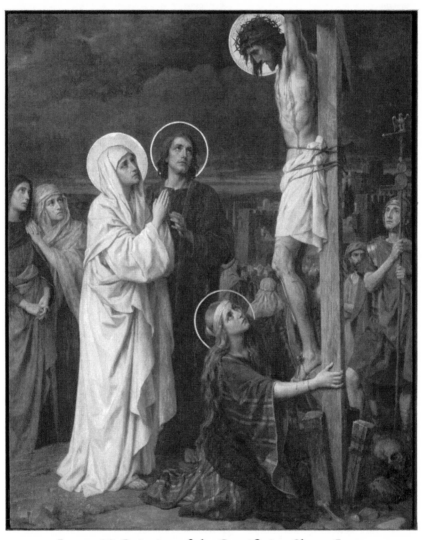

Image 20: Painting of the Crucifixion Shows Jesus Addressing His Mother from the Cross

CHAPTER 20:
JESUS SEES A WOMAN FROM THE CROSS

As reported in all four Gospels, Pilate handed Jesus over to be crucified. Mark's Gospel gives this detailed description:

> Then they led him out to crucify him. They compelled a passer-by who was coming in from the country, to carry his cross; it was Simon of Cyrene, the father of Alexander and Rufus. Then they brought Jesus to the place called Golgotha (which means the place of a skull). And they offered him wine mixed with Myrrh; but he did not take it. And they crucified him, and divided his clothes among them, casting lots to decide what each should take.

> It was nine o'clock in the morning when they crucified him. The inscription of the charge against him read, "The King of the Jews." And with him they crucified two bandits, one on his right, one on his left. Those who passed by derided him, shaking their heads and saying, "Aha! You who would destroy the Temple and build it in three days, save yourself, and come down from the cross!"[239]

> There were also women looking on from a distance; among them were Mary Magdalene, and Mary the mother of James the younger and of Joses, and Salome. These used to follow him and provided for him when he was in

---

[239] Op. cit., *NRSV*, Mark 15:20b–30, p. 54.

Galilee; and there were many other women who had come up with him to Jerusalem.[240]

All three Synoptic Gospels indicate that Jesus's female followers stood watching the crucifixion from a distance.

Only John claims that Jesus's mother, Mary, and an unnamed disciple—whom John labels "the one whom Jesus loved"—are at the foot of the Cross, close enough to hear Jesus address them. The presence of armed guards there would have dissuaded most onlookers from coming so close. John says:

> Meanwhile, standing near the cross of Jesus, were his mother, and his mother's sister, Mary the wife of Clopas, and Mary Magdalene. When Jesus saw his mother and the disciple whom he loved standing beside her, he said to his mother, "Woman, here is your son.' Then he said to the disciple, "Here is your mother." And from that hour the disciple took her into his own home.[241]

Guided Meditation

Imagine Jesus's grief-stricken mother watching her son die. She is close enough to hear his sighs and watch the sweat accumulate on his brow. This is the darkest day of her life.

---

240 Ibid. *NRSV,* Mark 15:40–41, p. 54.
241 Op. cit., *NRSV,* John 19:25b–27, p. 114.

Imagine how upset Jesus is to see his mother so close to the scene of his crucifixion. He is aware that she will become a childless widow when he dies.

Imagine that, as he faces his own death, Jesus is eager to arrange for her care. He calls to her and his beloved disciple and places them in each other's care.

Comments on the Gospel of John Story

The writer of the Gospel of John has placed Jesus's mother, Mary, at three significant events. In the story of the wedding at Cana, she is the first woman who is identified by name.[242] She is cited for her belief that Jesus can provide what is needed. [243] She requires no miracle to believe; she believes in his power before anyone or anything reveals who Jesus is and before he performs a miracle. John portrays her as the new Eve (whose name means "mother of all living things"), and she prompts Jesus to begin his work of redemption at the wedding at Cana. Mary Getty-Sullivan adds that the woman who calls for a miracle at a time when Jesus's "hour had not come" reappears at his final hour to represent the "perfect believer" whose faith and witness will lead to "a deeper faith for all who follow him."[244]

Mary's presence at the Cross is John's way of displaying her enduring faithfulness, a mark of a disciple. By commissioning his mother's care to his disciple, John is showing that Jesus has finished the work he came to do, a work that started and ended with his mother. At his death, Jesus's mother

---

[242] Op. cit., Thurston, p. 81.
[243] Ibid., Thurston, p. 82.
[244] Op cit, Getty-Sullivan, p. 222-223

becomes a childless widow, so John's Gospel enables her son to take care of his mother as his last act.

Mary Ann Getty-Sullivan suggests that John is presenting Jesus's mother Mary and the beloved disciple as "symbolic figures."[245] "Both are empowered to persevere" despite Jesus's death "because they recognize themselves as loved."[246] Getty-Sullivan adds that these exchanges between Jesus, his mother, and the beloved disciple are presented as signs that the church was created at the moment of Jesus's death.[247] This is the source from which the ancient church began to show Mary as the model for "right believing."

Elizabeth Johnson's book, *Truly Our Sister,* written in 2003, presents a compelling post-Vatican II theology that is "both critical of and deeply steeped in the Mary tradition."[248] She says:

> [The scene at the cross] conjures up all the anguish and
> desolation a woman could experience who had given birth
> to a child, loved that child, raised and taught that child,
> even tried to protect that child, only to have him executed
> in the worst imaginable way by the power of the state."[249]

Like Johnson, other scholars conclude that John offers the presence of the birth mother of Jesus as a reminder of the incarnation, and the beloved disciple represents the disciple whose love and works will extend the Gospel. Thus, the past and the future meet symbolically at the foot of the Cross.

I think it serves the purposes of the writer of the Gospel of John to place Mary at the Cross, to serve dramatically as the beginning and end

---

[245]   Op. cit., Getty-Sullivan, p. 228.

[246]   Ibid., Getty-Sullivan, p. 228.

[247]   Ibid., Getty-Sullivan, p. 230.

[248]   A quote from the National Catholic Reporter, which appears on the back cover of Johnson's book, *Truly Our Sister.*

[249]   Johnson, Elizabeth A., *Truly Our Sister,* pp. 293–294.

of his story about Jesus. It serves his goal to construct a Gospel that results in a belief that Jesus is the Son of God.

Is John's Story Believable?

Johnson, along with other biblical scholars, question whether the scene at the Cross, described by John's Gospel is "actually historical or whether its origin lies in the evangelist's 'symbolic imagination'" whereas "Jesus's death on the cross is clearly an historical event" as is "the presence of women at the cross.[250] She points to five Synoptic factors that count against the historicity of John's scene[251]:

1. "There is no mention in the Synoptic Gospels of the mother of Jesus being among the women at the cross."

2. "Luke, who places her in Jerusalem with the community of disciples at Pentecost, would likely have named her among the Galilean women if he knew that she was present at the crucifixion."

3. "The Gospels stress that all the male disciples fled or scattered which leaves little room for the continued presence of one believing, beloved male disciple."

4. The unnamed, beloved disciple "is utterly peculiar to John's Gospel."

5. "The symbolic theological importance of the crucifixion scene in John surfaces in the idea that at the end of his life Jesus brought into being a community in the very Spirit that flowed from him on the cross."

The Scene at the Cross Reported by the Synoptic Gospels

The Synoptic Gospels list several of Jesus's female followers at the Cross. The only woman who is reported to be present by both the Synoptic

---

[250] Op. cit., Johnson, p. 294
[251] Ibid., Johnson, p. 294

Gospels and the Gospel of John is Mary Magdalene. However, the Fourth Gospel is the only one in which Mary Magdalene is not placed first.

When Mark describes the death of Jesus, he says:

> When it was noon, darkness came over the whole land until three in the afternoon. At three o'clock Jesus cried out with a loud voice "Eloi, Eloi, lema sabachthani?" which means, "My God, my God, why have you forsaken me?"[252]

> Then Jesus gave a loud cry and breathed his last. And the curtain of the Temple was torn in two, from top to bottom. Now when the centurion, who stood facing him, saw that that in this way he breathed his last, he said, "Truly this man was God's Son!" There were also women looking on from a distance; among them were Mary Magdalene, and Mary the mother of James the younger and of Joses and Salome. These used to follow him and provided for him when he was in Galilee; and there were many other women who had come up with him to Jerusalem.[253]

Matthew's description of the scene of the cross is similar to Mark's:

> From noon on, darkness came over the whole land, until three in the afternoon. About three o'clock Jesus cried with a loud voice, "Eli, Eli, lema sabachthani?" that is "My God, my God, why have you forsaken me?"[254]

> Then Jesus cried again with a loud voice and breathed his last. At that moment the curtain of the Temple was

---

[252] Op. cit., *NRSV*, Mark 15:33-34, p. 54
[253] Ibid., *NRSV*, Mark 15:37-41, p. 54
[254] Op. cit., *NRSV*, Matthew 27:45-46, p. 33

torn in two, from top to bottom. The earth shook, and the rocks were split.[255]

Now when the centurion and those with him, who were keeping watch over Jesus, saw the earthquake and what took place, they were terrified and said, "Truly this man was God's Son!" Many women were also there, looking on from a distance; they had provided for him. Among them were Mary Magdalene, and Mary the mother of James and Joseph, and the mother of the sons of Zebedee.[256]

When Luke describes the women that were present at Jesus's death, they are not identified by their names. He makes no reference to individual women. He writes:

It was now about noon, and darkness came over the whole land until three in the afternoon, while the sun's light failed; the curtain of the Temple was torn in two. Then Jesus, crying with a loud voice, said, "Father, into your hands I commend my spirit." Having said this, he breathed his last. When the centurion saw what had taken place, he praised God and said, "Certainly this man was innocent." And when all the crowds who had gathered there for this spectacle saw what had taken place, they returned home. But all his acquaintances, including the women who had followed him from Galilee, stood at a distance, watching these things.[257]

---

[255] Ibid., *NRSV,* Matthew 27:50-51, p. 33

[256] Ibid., *NRSV,* Matthew 27:54-56, p. 33

[257] Op. cit., *NRSV,* Luke 23:44-49, p. 89

Conclusions

When Mark and Matthew's descriptions of the crucifixions are compared, Mary Magdalene is listed first by both of them. The identities of the other women are not as clear. Many suggest that the woman that Mark calls "Mary the mother of James the younger and of Joses" may be the same as Matthew's Mary, the mother of James and Joseph and that Salome, whom Mark identifies, is the same as Matthew's mother of the sons of Zebedee. So far, we cannot verify whether they are describing the same women.

None of the writers of the Synoptic Gospels name the mother of Jesus as one who is present at the Cross. Remembering that the Synoptic Gospels show that Jesus's mother did not understand or approve of the mission and ministry of Jesus suggests that her support developed later, after his death and resurrection, when the excitement of his disciples' encounters with the risen Christ gathered them all to receive the Holy Spirit at Pentecost (as Luke describes it in Acts). I agree with those who say that, had Luke known she was also at the Cross, he would have said so.

My Views of the Cross

The possibility that John's account of the Cross lacks historicity—and a growing awareness of John's apparent symbolism—have led me to develop a different view of the scene at the Cross. At first, John names Jesus's mother, his mother's sister, Mary (the wife of Clopas), and Mary Magdalene. Without knowing his sources, we may never know why he chose those four women. However, when he shifts his focus to Jesus's gaze and says that Jesus saw his mother and the disciple whom he loved standing beside her, it set the world of Christendom on a quest to find out who that was. I think it is very possible that Mary Magdalene is the disciple whom Jesus loved. The only reason we might think otherwise is John's use of the male pronoun.

My hypothesis rests on the published excerpts of several new translations of fragments from ancient texts that were not included in the official canons of the church, probably because they expressed unorthodox viewpoints. During the last decade, more and more scholars have examined these texts and their findings are eye-opening.[258] I find it very plausible that Magdalene and the beloved disciple are the same person based on the content of the Gospel of Mary Magdalene, where Peter says the following to Mary Magdalene:

> Sister, we know that the Teacher loved you differently from other women, tell us whatever you remember of any words he told you which we have not heard. Mary said to them: "I will speak to you of that which has not been given to you to hear. I had a vision of the Teacher, and I said to him, "Lord I see you now in this vision." He answered: "You are blessed, for the sight of me does not disturb you. There where is the *nous*, lies the treasure."[259]

Admittedly there is much controversy in Christian circles regarding these texts. Before you rush off and holler heretic at me, take some time to acquaint yourself with the portraits of Magdalene found in the noncanonical gospels. Because Mary Magdalene is the focus of the next chapter of this book, I will encourage you to follow along with me to better appreciate her.

I invite you to imagine the scene at the Cross and develop your own conclusions. Who do you think is the "beloved disciple"?

---

[258] Elaine Pagels, *Beyond Belief, The Secret Gospel of Thomas*, Karen L. King, *The Gospel of Mary Magdala,* and Jean-Yves Leloup, *The Gospel of Philip* and *The Gospel of Mary Magdalene* were my first introductions to these ancient texts.

[259] Leloup, Jean-Yves, *The Gospel of Mary Magdalene*, p. 31.

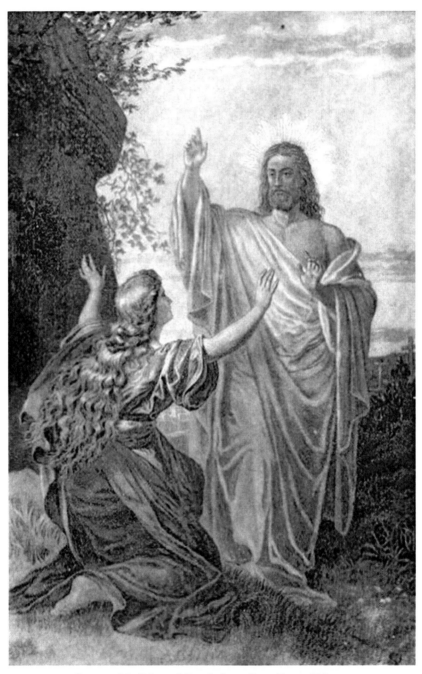

Image 21: Mary Magdalene Sees Jesus Risen

CHAPTER 21:
JESUS GREETS MARY
MAGDALENE AT THE TOMB

Despite the many voluptuous portrayals of Mary Magdalene you have seen, there is not a shred of evidence to support the claim that she was a prostitute. In fact, she was a significant companion of Jesus who shared in his ministry and stood by him until the very end.

However, in the sixth century, Pope Gregory I, also known as Pope Gregory the Great, erroneously combined the stories of the several women who anointed Jesus and attributed all of their actions to one woman: Mary Magdalene. In a sermon given in 597 AD, Pope Gregory said:

> She whom Luke calls the sinful woman, whom John calls Mary, we believe to be the Mary from whom seven demons were ejected according to Mark. And what did these seven demons signify if not all the vices? [...] It is clear, brothers that the woman previously used the unguent to perfume her flesh in forbidden acts. What she therefore displayed more scandalously, she was now offering to God in a more praiseworthy manner.[260]

Pope Gregory then tied the seven demons, said to have been banished by Jesus, to the seven deadly sins. His incorrect notion that Mary Magdalene was a prostitute, redeemed by Jesus, led artists and sculptors to depict her as a voluptuous woman who anoints Jesus with oils from an alabaster jar prior to the crucifixion. What Pope Gregory did by conflating four different stories about possibly four different women and naming *all* the

---

[260] Gregory, *Homily 33.*

219

women Mary Magdalene was to demean the character of a loyal disciple and contrast her to the beatified virgin mother of Jesus. Most of us grew up believing that Mary Magdalene was a repentant woman whose conversion was synonymous with her healing.

Biblical scholars outside of Rome eventually differentiated these women into Mary of Bethany, the sister of Martha and Lazarus whom John claims anointed Jesus; the unnamed woman, who was a redeemed sinner who bathed Jesus's feet with her tears and anointed them with the ointment she carried in an alabaster jar (as described by Luke); the unnamed woman who anointed the head of Jesus described by Mark and Matthew; and Mary of Magdala, who brought oils to the tomb. If you wonder why this is still news in many circles, it is because it wasn't until Vatican II, in the second half of the twentieth century, that the Roman Catholic hierarchy disentangled these other women from Mary Magdalene. This disentanglement allowed her to be seen as the extraordinary apostle that she was, and the first to be commissioned by the risen Christ to tell others the good news of his resurrection.

If this information is new to you, you may be shocked to hear that Mary Magdalene was not a healed prostitute and that this image of her is untrue!

Elizabeth Moltmann-Wendel was one of the first women to express her outrage over this mislabeling and the hundreds of years that passed before the image of the Magdalene stopped being disparaged.[261] Unlike Jesus's mother, Mary, Moltmann-Wendel attests, Mary Magdalene was the one who stood by Jesus and valued him above all else.

---

[261] Op. cit., Moltmann-Wendel, pp. 64–66.

Reflection Question

Do you need to take time to examine how this corrected information changes your view of Mary Magdalene and how you feel about the biases that prevailed for so long?

Luke's Contribution to Mary Magdalene's False Image

Luke's introduction of Mary Magdalene as healed of demons contributed to Pope Gregory's misconceptions. Luke wrote the following:

> Soon afterwards [Jesus] went on through cities and villages, proclaiming and bringing the good news of the [realm] of God. The Twelve were with him, as well as some women who had been cured of evil spirits and infirmities: Mary, called Magdalene, from whom seven demons had gone out, and Joanna, the wife of Herod's steward Chuza, and Susanna and many others, who provided for them out of their resources.[262]

Cynthia Bourgeault has questioned Luke's conclusions that Mary was healed of evil spirits because his is the only Gospel that says this. Many believe that a similar reference in Mark 16:9 was added later to be consistent with Luke. Because there is no mention of her infirmity in either Mathew or John (or any of the noncanonical gospels), I assume that her belief in and commitment to Jesus's teaching are sufficient to explain her

---

[262] Op. cit., *NRSV,* LUKE 8:1–3, p. 67.

devotion. If that is true, that would make her devotion to Jesus equal to or ahead of the male disciples in comprehending their teacher—a notion that the ecclesial establishment might oppose then and now. Cynthia Bourgeault has even suggested that Luke's mention of a healing of demons may have been included at the time of his writing in order to discredit her and diminish her perceived value.[263]

At this point, there is no way to determine whether Mary of Magdela was the recipient of Jesus's miraculous healing powers. There is considerable evidence, however, that she later became a leader in the believing community, and it is that leadership that I have chosen to focus on.

Mary Magdalene

Who, then, is Mary of Magdala? The town of Magdala no longer exists; it is believed to have been a commercial town on Lake Gennesaret, where fishing and trade flourished.[264]

In truth, we know little about her—only that she became a follower. We don't know her age or the nature of her appearance. We do know that she was one of a group of women and a leader among them. Nothing is said of her in the Scriptures between the healing mentioned in Luke and the crucifixion, unless she is the unnamed woman who anoints the head of Jesus, described in Chapter 17 of this book.

She holds the privileged position of being the one to whom Jesus first appears and the one to whom he gives the task of telling the others that he has risen. Until he calls her by name, Mary doesn't recognize Jesus outside the tomb. It is too soon for her to understand how his death and resurrection have changed things. Yet the task Jesus gives her and the subsequent formation of a new community of believers depend upon her.

---

263 Op. cit., Bourgeault, p. 14.
264 Op. cit., Moltmann-Wendel, p. 68.

After Jesus is seized in the garden of Gethsemane and taken before the Jewish authorities, his male disciples flee in fear that what has happened to him might happen to them as well. When the once-boastful Peter is recognized as one of Jesus's disciples, he denies knowing him and then hides with the rest of the men. In contrast, Mary Magdalene is identified by name as a witness to these three key events: Jesus's crucifixion, his burial, and the discovery that his tomb was empty.

Mark 15:40, Matthew 27:56, and John 19:25 all mention Mary Magdalene as a witness to the crucifixion. Crucifixion is a horrific way to die. It is excruciatingly slow. Bystanders gathered to watch, and some taunted Jesus, expecting him to use his power to get down from the Cross. They relished the gruesome spectacle. Armed guards were present to ensure and then validate that death had occurred. And then, there were these women who devoted their lives to Jesus watching from a distance. I don't think they were willing to let him die alone. Their love compels them to remain and abide with him.

Guided Meditation

Imagine Mary Magdalene standing near enough to the Cross to watch her beloved teacher die. Imagine her seeing his pain and hearing the jeers of the onlookers.

If you have been present when someone you loved was dying, do your memories of that event help you appreciate what Mary Magdalene felt like?

Take time to remember here, your experiences in the presence of someone you loved who was dying.

Comments

The sacred process of dying is unforgettable. It is the process of life becoming extinguished. When your heart is full of compassion, there is no other place you would rather be.[265]

Mary Magdalene Is Present when Jesus's Body Is Laid in a Tomb

Mark tells us that, on that same day, Joseph of Arimathea, a respected member of the council and a disciple of Jesus, went to Pilate and asked for the body of Jesus. When Pilate learns that Jesus is already dead, he grants the body to Joseph:[266]

> Then Joseph bought a linen cloth and taking down the body, wrapped it in the linen cloth and laid it in a tomb that had been hewn out of the rock. He then rolled a stone against the door of the tomb. Mary Magdalene and Mary the mother of Joses saw where the body was laid.[267]

Mary Magdalene and those who accompanied her needed to know where the body of Jesus was laid so that they could return after the Sabbath to anoint the body with spices in preparation for the final burial.

---

[265] See Megory Anderson, *Sacred Dying,* for ways to embrace the end of life. Roseville, CA, Prima Publishing, 2001.

[266] Op. cit., *NRSV,* Mark 15: 42–45, p. 54.

[267] Ibid., *NRSV,* Mark 15: 46–47.

<u>Mary Magdalene Arrives at the Tomb</u>

There is considerable variance in the way the four Gospel writers describe what happened at the tomb. I will present them in the order in which they were written.

The Gospel of Mark gives us the *earliest* account of what Mary Magdalene found when she returned the next day to the tomb:

> When the Sabbath was over, Mary Magdalene and Mary the mother of James, and Salome bought spices, so that they might go and anoint him. And very early on the first day of the week, when the sun had risen, they went to the tomb. They had been saying to one another "Who will roll away the stone for us from the entrance to the tomb?" When they looked up, they saw that the stone, which was very large, had been rolled back. As they entered the tomb, they saw a young man, dressed in a white robe, sitting on the right side; and they were alarmed. But he said to them, "Do not be alarmed; you are looking for Jesus of Nazareth, who was crucified. He has been raised; he is not here. Look, there is the place they laid him. But go, tell his disciples and Peter that he is going ahead of you to Galilee; there you will see him, just as he told you." So they went out and fled from the tomb, for terror and amazement had seized them; and they said nothing to anyone, for they were afraid.[268]

Thirty-six hours after seeing Jesus die and be buried, Mary of Magdala finds the tomb empty. The earliest version of Mark's gospel ends abruptly there. The remaining verses were added later. The women do not do what the messenger in white commands. They flee the tomb in terror and astonishment and say nothing. We are left in a state of expectancy.

---

[268] Ibid., *NRSV*, Mark 16:1–8, pp. 54–55.

Matthew's version of finding the tomb empty is similar: there, the women are greeted by "an angel of the Lord, descending from heaven" who "came and rolled back the stone and sat on it. His appearance was like lightning and his clothing white as snow."[269] Jesus appears to them also, and he corroborates the angel's message. This is Matthew's account:

> The angel said to the women, "Do not be afraid. I know that you are looking for Jesus who was crucified. He is not here; for he has been raised, as he said. Come, see the place where he lay. Then go quickly and tell his disciples. He has been raised from the dead, and indeed he is going ahead of you to Galilee; there you will see him. This is my message for you." So they left the tomb quickly with fear and great joy, and ran to tell his disciples. Suddenly Jesus met them and said, "Greetings!" And they came to him, took hold of his feet and worshiped him. Then Jesus said to them, "Do not be afraid; go and tell my brothers to go to Galilee; there they will see me."[270]

In Luke's Gospel, when the women find the stone rolled away and there is no body in the tomb, they see two men in dazzling clothes standing beside them. The women are terrified and bow their faces to the ground, but the men say the following to them:

> "Why do you look for the living among the dead? He is not here, but he has risen. Remember how he told you, while he was still in Galilee, that the Son of [Humanity] must be handed over to sinners, and be crucified, and on the third day rise again." Then they remembered his words, and returning from the tomb, they told all this to the eleven and to all the rest. Now it was Mary Magdalene, Joanna, Mary the mother of James and the other women with them who told this to the apostles. But these words

---

[269] Op cit, *NRSV*, Matthew 28:2–3, p. 33.
[270] Ibid., *NRSV*, Matthew 28:3–10, pp. 33–34.

seemed to them an idle tale and they did not believe them. But Peter got up and ran to the tomb; stooping and looking in, he saw the linen cloths by themselves; then he went home, amazed at what had happened.[271]

The Gospel account with which we are most familiar is John's because it is the text used to describe Jesus's passion on Palm Sunday and Good Friday. However, it is the last one written and contains many details that do not appear in the other three. They are as follows:

1. Joseph of Arimathea is accompanied by Nicodemus, and together they wrap the body with a mixture of myrrh and aloes in linen cloths, in accord with Jewish burial customs.[272]

2. The two men lay the covered body in a new tomb in the garden where he was crucified. Countryman reminds us that both men "belong to that group of powerful people who believed in Jesus but would not admit it because they loved human glory more than the glory that God gives."[273]

3. When Mary Magdalene discovers that the stone is rolled away, she runs to Simon Peter and the other disciple – "the one whom Jesus loved" – and says, "They have taken the Lord out of the tomb, and we do not know where they have laid him."[274]

4. Peter and the other disciple race toward the tomb. "The other disciple outran Peter and reached the tomb first. He bends down to look in and saw the linen wrappings lying there, but did not go in. Then Simon Peter came, following him, and went into the tomb. He saw the linen wrappings lying there.[275] Then the other disciple, who reached the tomb first, also went in, and he saw and believed;

---

[271] Op cit, *NRSV*, Luke 24:5b–12, p. 90.
[272] Op. cit., *NRSV*, John 19:38–41.
[273] Op cit, Countryman, p. 132.
[274] Op. cit., *NRSV*, John 20:1-2.
[275] Ibid., *NRSV*, John 20:2, p. 114.

for as yet they did not understand the scripture, that he must rise from the dead. Then the disciples returned to their homes."[276]

It is John's description of the mournful Mary Magdalene that stirs our emotion and captures our hearts. The intensity of her grief corresponds with the depth of her devotion and loyalty to Jesus. John wrote the following:

> But Mary stood weeping outside the tomb. As she wept, she bent over to look into the tomb, and she saw two angels in white, sitting where the body of Jesus had been lying, one at the head and the other at the feet. They said to her, "Woman, why are you weeping?" She said to them, "They have taken away my Lord, and I do not know where they have laid him."

> When she had said this, she turned around and saw Jesus standing there, but she did not know that it was Jesus. Jesus said to her, "Woman, why are you weeping? Whom are you looking for?" Supposing him to be the gardener, she said to him, "Sir, if you have carried him away, tell me where you have laid him, and I will take him away." Jesus said to her, "Mary!" She turned and said to him in Hebrew, "Rabbouni!" (which means Teacher). Jesus said to her, "Do not hold on to me, because I have not yet ascended to [The Almighty One]. But go to my brothers and say to them, "I am ascending to [The Almighty], to my God and your God." Mary Magdalene went and announced to the disciples, "I have seen the Lord" and she told them that he had said these things to her.[277]

---

[276] Ibid., *NRSV*, John 20:8–10, p. 114.
[277] Ibid., *NRSV*, John 20:11–18, pp. 114–115.

Guided Meditation

Imagine the greeting that takes place between Mary of Magdala and the risen Jesus. See him stop her impulse to embrace him.

Imagine her surprise and elation to find him alive!

Imagine Mary Magdalene's reaction when Jesus commissions her to spread the good news of his resurrection by saying, "Go to my brothers and tell them."[278]

Comments

In the early days of the Eastern Orthodox Church, Mary Magdalene was given the title "The Apostle to the Apostles." They held her in high regard from the beginning. They did not believe that she had been a prostitute.

None of the Gospel passages provide many clues as to Jesus's attitude toward Mary of Magdala. Still, we can deduce that he was not surprised by her appearance at the empty tomb, that he trusted her to tell the others, and that he treated her as an equal to the male disciples.

Mary Magdalene's preferential position (and her conflict with the male disciples) is evident in the Gospel of John. According to John, when the

---

[278] Op. cit., *MSG*, John 20:17, p. 1967.

women reported the resurrection, the men disregarded what they said and required proof from their own experience of the empty tomb.

Mary Magdalene's behavior at the tomb demonstrates that she was a devoted disciple who understood the victory attained by the resurrection. One great gift of the noncanonical gospels is that they show Mary Magdalene to have the deepest understanding of the teachings of Jesus and the best ability to live out what she understands. Cynthia Bourgeault's comments on the tomb en are worth noting.

> It is *love* standing at the foot of the cross, *love* following the small entourage that takes his body from the cross and places it in the tomb, *love* holding vigil when everyone else has gone home.[279]

> And it is *love* that remains there for those entire three days (for where else is there to go?)[280]

Bourgeault adds that, on the morning of the resurrection, the Magdalene utters "an astonished cry of "Rabboni." She notes:

> The Magdalene recognizes that he has, indeed, ended where he began. She is the last person he sees before he leaves the human realm and the first person he sees upon returning. Together again in that garden [...] they once again gaze into each other's eyes, exchanging their unspoken joy. Then with a forceful "Go and tell the others" he sends her forth.[281]

These descriptions of their relationship are so awe-inspiring that I want you to experience them, too.

---

[279] Ibid., Bourgeault, p. 153–154.
[280] Ibid., Bourgeault, p. 154.
[281] Ibid., Bourgeault, pp. 156. Here, she draws heavily on Lynn Bauman, ed. *The Gospel of Thomas: the Wisdom of the Twin*, p. 225.

Reflection Questions

Hear Jesus call you now, as he called Mary of Magdala. He is giving *you* the job of telling the others that the Lord has risen. Notice that Jesus is keeping his promise to be with us. Do *you* wonder why Jesus would choose you to represent him?

Do you hesitate?

What can you tell others based on your own experiences?

Do you wonder whether anyone will believe you?

Do you question the validity of your own experience?

Think of the Magdalene: she had nothing more than her experience to share—no divinity degree and no special status in the community. Once bidden, she simply did as Jesus asked: she shared her experience with those who would listen. And because of her, many believed! We, too, are witnesses with experiences to share. What do you have to tell others?

<u>Conclusions</u>

Mary Magdalene cared enough to be there at each of those critical moments in the life of Jesus. He asked her to tell the others that he had risen and would meet them all in Galilee.

Equally important is the fact that we, too, are witnesses of the risen Jesus. Like Mary of Magdala, Jesus calls us each by name and tells us to go and tell others our good news. Mary Magdalene's life was radically changed by her encounters with Jesus, and our lives can be changed radically by him as well!

Each of us has been blessed by God with our unique experiences and gifts. Alone, we may be able to do little, but with God's love and empowerment, we can do so much more than we could ever imagine. Go forth now, in the name of Jesus, the Christ.

CHAPTER 22: CONCLUSIONS

In each of these encounters, we see a man who demonstrates that every person is worthy of his attention. He is quick to size up the woman who stands before him, and despite any initial hesitancy, he responds with empathy, compassion, and concern. It is through his humanness that he reveals the magnitude of God's love.

He commends the service of these women and their intentionality. He is changed by their perseverance and persistence. He is touched by their humility and their hardships. And he encourages and praises their leadership. His actions and responses allow us to see how really impressive these women are. It is no wonder that they have been remembered all these years. They offer us positive role models to identify with and emulate.

Some of these women are the only figures in the Gospels to change the mind of Jesus. Though resistant at first, he becomes receptive to opinions that differ from his own. He is moved to gift the wedding couple at Cana with more wine and to heal those who stand outside the circle of the children of Abraham. He offers a vision of a new world, one in which no one is insignificant. It is a world in which even women have a place of respect, where no one misuses their power over another and there is food for everyone.

In story after story, we see him giving freedom: freedom from afflictions and infirmities, freedom from unworkable lives, freedom from sin, and even freedom from death. With courage and certainty, he challenges the Mosaic Law when strict adherence to it imposes heavy burdens on people.

Much of Jesus's teaching is based on these human examples. Many of these stories illustrate love: God's love, parental love, mutual friendship, and love for a stranger in need (which we now call neighbor love). It is because Jesus begins where we do that he can take us where he is going. He provides us with a model of a completed human being,[282] what others call "a true son of humanity" or "living spirit." And it is his humanness that guides us on our own paths.[283]

He displays such extraordinary power at work in him that he is compared to the God who sent him.

A recent review of the second and most recent edition of The Revised Common Lectionary: Episcopal Edition, published in 2006, reveals that the gospel lessons chosen for each Sunday now includes all but three of my stories (for the first time), which gives women an acknowledged place in the ministry of Jesus.

The story of the adulteress woman, which has been a source of discomfort to church authorities who fear that it encourages recklessness and sin by women is not included among the chosen gospels. In reality, its ethical message is vital: Jesus said that if you wish to accuse others, you must be without reproach yourself. In so doing, he highlights the importance of seeing ourselves as sinners, which can heal our judgmental hearts and enable us to regard others with compassion and love. The story continues to witness to the One who redeemed the life of both the woman and her accusers.

The second story that does not appear in the Revised Common Lectionary is the dream of Pilate's wife, which only appears in the Gospel of Matthew. That Gospel is not used on Good Friday; only John's account is used all three years, a fact that I hope to see change.

---

[282] Op. cit., Bourgeault, pp. 119–121.

[283] The quest for *anthropos*, "the completed human Being" is mentioned in the Gospel of Philip more than ten times in terms that correspond exactly with the Gospel of Thomas.

The third story you will not hear on a Sunday is the story of Jesus being found in the temple at age twelve. I will lobby for its inclusion in liturgies of confirmation and ordination.

More than forty years ago, I wrote a dissertation on the significant impact of recognizing one's similarity to others in sensitivity training, therapy, and encounter groups.[284] My research showed that group members who discovered their similarity to other members, developed enhanced self-esteem, a sense of being worthwhile, reassurance, and hope. If others were successful in areas that were difficult for them, they were encouraged and gained a renewed commitment to their goals. If they surpassed some of the others, they grew in self-confidence. Others' insights contributed to their own self-understanding. After all these years of studying these Gospel women, I am surprised to discover that the findings of my dissertation research find a parallel in the stories of the women who knew Jesus. It is impossible to avoid seeing parts of ourselves in them.

Whether or not you have taken the time to identify your personal connection to any of these women, I urge you to think about each of them now. Ask yourself the following: who among these women reminds me most of myself? And then let the wisdom that results from that recognized similarity arise in your consciousness.

Consider the following:

The young Mary who responds positively to the angel's reassurance and agrees to birth God's child.

Mary, as a mother of a twelve-year-old child, is upset by her son's disappearance and disapproves of his independent actions, which she fails to understand.

---

[284] Ring, Bonnie, *Recognized Similarity: An Investigation of Significant Events Reported by Encounter Group Participants,* an unpublished doctoral dissertation, Boston University, 1972.

Peter's mother-in-law, who jumps up after Jesus heals her and shows her vitality by serving all of them.

The mother of Jesus, whose confidence in his ability to miraculously produce wine leads her to press him to do just that.

The woman with a hemorrhage, whose desperation and faith result in her healing when she touches the hem of Jesus's garment.

The twelve-year-old daughter of Jairus, whom Jesus brings back to life.

The forthright Samaritan woman who meets Jesus at Jacob's well.

The mother of Jesus, who thinks he is out of his mind.

The grief-stricken widow from Nain, whose son Jesus brings back to life.

The sassy Syro-Phoenician woman, whose challenges cause Jesus to change his mind and heal her daughter—thus extending his ministry beyond the people of Israel.

Mary of Bethany, who listens attentively as Jesus teaches (as all of us are encouraged to do).

Martha of Bethany, who, as the hostess, is frantic about many things and complains to Jesus about her sister, who is listening to him.

The bent-over woman, who was healed by Jesus so that she could stand up straight and see him clearly.

The unnamed woman accused of adultery who is sent on her way when none of her accusers are themselves without sin.

Martha of Bethany, who prods Jesus to raise her brother, Lazarus, from death and acknowledges that Jesus is the Messiah.

Martha's sister, Mary, whose tears arouse Jesus's tears and prompt him to act.

The Mother of Zebedee's sons, who requests privileges for them and learns about true discipleship.

The generous, poor widow whom Jesus praises.

The woman who anoints Jesus's head with oil, thus proclaiming that he is the Anointed One.

Mary of Bethany, who anoints Jesus's feet with tenderness before his death.

The repentant woman, whose gratitude leads her to anoint Jesus, according to Luke.

The wife of Pilate who warns her husband after having a disturbing dream about Jesus.

Mary Magdalene, whose presence at the cross and at the tomb is a sign of her loyalty and devotion.

Make a check mark alongside the stories that impacted you the most. Remember their stories, recall the feelings that their experiences evoked in you, and let the Holy Spirit reveal even more to you about yourself.

When I complete my spiritual memoir, I will publish my list too.

Jesus sought always to heal others and make them whole in body, mind, and spirit. In my life, Psychotherapy, Spiritual Direction and Interplay have been extraordinary resources for attaining that wholeness.[285] Whatever we do, seeking our own wholeness should be our first priority. What matters to Jesus is not who we are, but how we live our lives. If you align your heart with his and follow in his path of compassion and integrity, you can become all that God intends for you to be. What you are is God's gift to you; what you make of yourself is your gift to God.

I hope your journey with these women has been rewarding. It has been a joy for me to know and love them all these years. They are our sisters. I look forward to hearing about your experience with this book.

Bonnie Ring
August 2015

---

[285] Interplay is an international program of body wisdom, improvisational dance, play, and storytelling that lets your heart speak. Their site is www.Interplay.org.

LIST OF ILLUSTRATIONS

Image 1. *Padua – Painting of Jesus and Samaritan at well.*
Credit: sedmak; Thinkstockphotos; Item number: 517467607; Collection: iStock

Image 2. *Mary places Jesus in a manger.*
Copyright 2003, 2013 La Vista Church of Christ, La Vista, Nebraska.
The Boys in the Bible by Hartwell James.
Published by Henry Altemus Company, 1905, 1916.

Image 3. *Jesus in the Temple Discussing His Father's Business.*
Copyright 2003, 2013 La Vista Church of Christ, La Vista, Nebraska.
Standard Bible Story Readers, Book Two by Lillie A. Faris.
Illustrated by O. A. Stemler and Bess Bruce Cleaveland.
The Standard Publishing Company, 1925.

Image 4. *Peter's Mother-in-Law was healed.*
Copyright 2003, 2013 La Vista Church of Christ, La Vista, Nebraska.
Standard Bible Story Readers, Book Two by Lillie A. Faris.
Illustrated by O. A. Stemler and Bess Bruce Cleaveland.
The Standard Publishing Company. 1925.

Image 5. *Jesus Changes Water into Wine.*
Copyright 2003, 2013 La Vista Church of Christ, La Vista, Nebraska.
Treasures of the Bible, Chapters 26–31 (Jesus's Ministry)
by Henry Davenport Northrop, D.D. International Publishing Company, 1894.

Image 6. *Woman with an issue of blood touches Jesus's garment.*
Copyright 2003, 2013 La Vista Church of Christ, La Vista, Nebraska.
The Children's Friend: Pictures and Stories of the Life of Jesus
by Mrs. Adelaide Bee Evans.
Review and Herald Publishing Association, 1911, 1928.

Image 7. *Jesus raising the daughter of Jairus.*
Credit: Photos.com; Thinkstockphotos; Item number: 92818597;
Collection: Photos.com

Image 8. *Jesus Speaks with a Samaritan Woman.*
Credit: Steven Wynn; Thinkstockphotos; Item number: 118365637;
Collection: iStock

Image 9. *Jesus teaching on the Seashore.*
Credit: Photos.com; Thinkstockphotos; Item number: 92822090;
Collection: Photos.com

Image 10. *Jesus raises the Widow of Nain's son.*
Copyright 2003, 2013 La Vista Church of Christ, La Vista, Nebraska.
Standard Bible Story Readers Book Six by Lillie A. Faris.
Illustrated by O. A. Stemler and Bess Bruce Cleaveland.
The Standard Publishing Company, 1929.
(Special thanks to Linda Hubbard who donated this book so pictures could
be used on the website.)

Image 11. *A Greek Woman Begs Jesus to Heal her Daughter.*
Copyright 2003, 2013 La Vista Church of Christ, La Vista, Nebraska.
The Children's Friend: Pictures and Stories of the Life of Jesus
by Mrs. Adelaide Bee Evans.
Review and Herald Publishing Association, 1911, 1928.

Image 12. *Jesus Christ at the Home of Mary and Martha.*
Credit: Steven Wynn; Thinkstockphotos; Item number: 114155425;
Collection: iStock

Image 13. *Jesus Heals an Elderly Woman.*
Credit: Steven Wynn; Thinkstockphotos; Item Number 118459392;
Collection: iStock

Image 14. *Rendering of Jesus defending The Woman Taken in Adultery.*
Credit: Photos.com; Thinkstockphotos; Item number: 92846592;
Collection: Photos.com

Image 15. *Padua – Painting of the Resurrection of Lazarus.*
Credit: sedmak Thinkstockphotos; Item number: 517424443; Collection:
iStock;

Image 16. *Jesus Answers the Mother of the Sons of Zebedee and the Disciples.*
Copyright 2003, 2013 La Vista Church of Christ, La Vista, Nebraska.
Standard Bible Story Reader, Book Six by Lillie A, Faris
Illustrated by O. A. Stemler and Bess Bruce Cleaveland.
The Standard Publishing Company, 1929.
(Special thanks to Linda Hubbard who donated this book so pictures could
be used on the website.)

Image 17. *The Widow Gave All She Had.*
Copyright 2003, 2013 La Vista Church of Christ, La Vista, Nebraska.
Standard Bible Story Reader, Book Six by Lillie A. Faris.
Illustrated by O. A. Stemler and Bess Bruce Cleaveland.
The Standard Publishing Company, 1929.
(Special thanks to Linda Hubbard who donated this book so pictures could
be used on the website.)

Image 18. *A Woman Anoints Jesus's Head.*
Copyright 2003, 2013 La Vista Church of Christ, La Vista, Nebraska.
Standard Bible Story Reader, Book Six by Lillie A. Faris.
Illustrated by O. A. Stemler and Bess Bruce Cleaveland.
The Standard Publishing Company, 1929.
(Special thanks to Linda Hubbard who donated this book so pictures could
be used on the website.)

Image 19. *Art depicting Jesus Before Pilate.*
Credit: Photos.com; Thinkstockphotos; Item number 92832140;
Collection: iStock

Image 20. *Antwerp – Crucifixion in Cathedral of Our Lady.*
Credit: sedmak; Thinkstockphotos; Item number 458577861; Collection: iStock Editorial

Image 21. *Mary Magdalene Sees Jesus Risen.*
Copyright 2003, 2013 La Vista Church of Christ, La Vista, Nebraska.
Treasures of the Bible, Chapters 32-33 by Henry Davenport Northrop, D.D. International Publishing Company, 1894.

BIBLIOGRAPHY

Athans, Mary Christine. *In Quest of the Jewish Mary*. Maryknoll: Orbis Books, 2013.

Anderson, Megory. *Sacred Dying*. Roseville: Prima Publishing, 2001.

Ashcroft, Mary Ellen. *Spirited Women*. Minneapolis: Augsberg Fortress, 2000.

Barrett, C. K. *The Gospel According to St. John, Second Edition*. Philadelphia: Westminster Press, 1978.

Bauckham, Richard. *Gospel Women*. Grand Rapids, MICH: William B. Eerdman's Publishing Company, 2002.

Bauman, Lynn C., and Ward J. Bauman and Cynthia Bourgeault. *The Luminous Gospels: Thomas, Mary Magdalene and Philip*. Telephone, Texas: Praxis Publishing, 2008.

Binz, Stephen J. *Women of the Gospels*. Grand Rapids, Brazo Press, 2011.

Bourgeault, Cynthia. *The Meaning of Mary Magdalene*. Boston: Shambala Publications, 2010.

Borg, Marcus. *Meeting Jesus Again for the First Time*, San Francisco: Harper Collins, 1994.

Brown, Raymond E. *The Gospel According to John I-XII*. Garden City: Doubleday, 1966.

Brown, Raymond E. *The Epistles of John*. Garden City: Doubleday, 1982.

Chilton, Bruce. *Mary Magdalene: A Biography*. New York: Doubleday, 2005.

Countryman, L. William. *The Mystical Way in the Fourth Gospel, Revised Edition*. Valley Forge: Trinity Press International, 1994.

Flanagan, Neal M. *The Gospel According to John and the Johanine Epistles*. Collegeville: Liturgical Press, 1983, 1989.

Fuchs, Lucy. *We Were There, Women in the New Testament*. New York: ALBA HOUSE, 1993.

Gench, Frances Taylor. *Back to the Well, Women's Encounters with Jesus in the Gospels*. Louisville, KY: John Knox Press, 2004.

Getty-Sullivan, Mary Ann. *Women in the New Testament*. Collegeville: Liturgical Press, 2001.

Johnson, Elizabeth A. *Truly Our Sister*. London: Bloomsbury Publishing, LLC, 2003.

Kalas, J. Ellsworth. *Strong Was Her Faith*. Nashville: Abingdon Press, 2007.

Kimbrough, Marjorie L. *She is Worthy, Encounters with Biblical Women*. Nashville: Abingdon Press, 1994.

Leloup, Jean-Yves. *The Gospel of Mary Magdalene*. Rochester, VT: Inner Traditions International and Bear Co., 2002.

Leloup, Jean-Yves. *The Gospel of Philip*. Rochester, VT: Inner Traditions International and Bear Co., 2004.

Moltmann-Wendel. *Women Around Jesus*. Crossroads Press, 1990.

Newsom, Carol A., Sharon H. Ringe and Jacqueline E. Lapsley (Eds.) *Women's Bible Commentary, revised and updated*. Louisville, KY: Westminster John Knox Press, 1992, 1998, 2012.

Pearson, Helen Bruch. *Do What You Have the Power to Do*, Nashville: Upper Room Books, 1992.

Redding, David A. *Lives He Touched*. New York: Harper Collins, 1978.

Reid, Barbara E. *Choosing the Better Part? Women in the Gospel of Luke*. Collegeville, MN: Liturgical Press, 1996.

Reuther, Rosemary Radford. *Mary – The Feminine Face of God*. Louisville, KY: Westminster John Knox Press, 1977.

Septien, Pia. *Women of the New Testament Their Lives, Our* Hope. Liguori, MO: Liguori Publications, 2012.

Shussler Fiorenza, Elisabeth. *But She Said, Feminist Practices of Biblical Interpretation*. Boston: Beacon Press, 1992.

Smith, Dennis and Michael E. Williams (Eds.). *The Storytellers Companion to the Bible, Volume 13: New Testament Women*. Nashville: Abingdon Press, 1999.

Swidler, Leonard. *Jesus was a Feminist*. London: Sheed & Ward, 2007.

Thurston, Bonnie. *Women in the New Testament*. Eugene, OR: Wipf & Stock Publishers, 1998.

Volo, James M. *The Women Who Knew Jesus: Female Role Models in Early Christianity*.

Williamson, Lamar Jr. *Interpretation: A Bible Commentary for Teaching and Preaching*. Louisville, KY: Westminster John Knox Press, 1983.

Young, Brad H. *New Testament Studies, 41:* "Save the Adulteress Ancient Jewish Responsa in the Gospels." Cambridge, England: Cambridge University Press, 1995.

Zimmer, Mary. *Sister Images, Guided Meditations from the Stories of Biblical Women*. Nashville: Abingdon Press, 1993.

CPSIA information can be obtained at www.ICGtesting.com
Printed in the USA
LVOW07*0011090816

499580LV00003B/11/P